The Beauty
of the
Outdoor World

Happy Valentines Day '76
Love from all the Switzers
to all the Maxeys

The Beauty
of the
Outdoor World

Published by
Outdoor World
Waukesha, Wisconsin

COUNTRY BEAUTIFUL: *Publisher & Editorial Director:* Michael P. Dineen; *Executive Editor:* Robert L. Polley; *Senior Editors:* Kenneth L. Schmitz, James H. Robb; *Art Director:* Buford Nixon; *Associate Editors:* D'Arlyn Marks, John M. Nuhn; *Editorial Assistants:* Kay Kundinger, Nancy Backes; *Art Assistant:* Tom McCann; *Production Manager:* Donna Griesemer; *Administration:* Brett E. Gries; *Editorial Secretary:* Jane E. Boyd.

Country Beautiful Corporation is a wholly owned subsidiary of Flick-Reedy Corporation: *President:* Frank Flick; *Vice President and General Manager:* Michael P. Dineen; *Treasurer and Secretary:* August Caamano.

Frontispiece: Early spring apple blossom. Photo by Paul E. Taylor.

"Creatures of the Night" on page 89 reprinted by permission of Reader's Digest, copyright 1970.
"The Sad Decline of the Alligator" on page 102 reprinted by permission of Reader's Digest, copyright 1969.

CONTENTS

PORTFOLIO-
PATTERNS IN NATURE

*L*et man learn from the Spider. Strand by silky strand he manufactures his web, undefectibly laid out and proportioned . . . equal to the chore the spider has for it. Nature offers many free classes to those who take the patience to sit in on its demonstration lectures.

—McDaniel

The subject here is one available to everyone: raindrops on the tips of white pine needles. Focus is deliberately shallow in order to keep the attention in one area only.

Abstracts

By Jerome Drown
Photography by the Author

It all began on a warm Sunday in November. I put a closeup attachment on the camera and began to focus on tiny things I had never really seen before. This was the day I learned how to make abstract nature photographs, using just the gentle forms of leaves and fleeting darts of light. The basic tools are simple. You must have a single-lens reflex camera as the recording instrument, a closeup lens as the probe, and a feeling for equations of form and light. Finally, you must get out and explore the underworld of beauty and activity among the twisting blades of grass, the curling tendrils of small vines, the many leaf forms of weeds, shifting images in and out of focus until a pleasing arrangement is found.

Weeds form the subject, but the photographer's eye forms the picture. The camera is simply the recording instrument. This is an extreme close-up of grasses and weeds in a summer field. The tendrils of saw-brier vines become an integral part of the picture. Corners are blurred by leaves held close to the lens.

Photographer Drown has a water oak in his front yard, which is one of his favorite subjects. Here a shaft of sunlight strikes the base of a leaf from behind and brings out reds and golds that were hidden from the naked eye. The blurred edges are simply an optical effect achieved by careful use of selective focus.

Abstracts

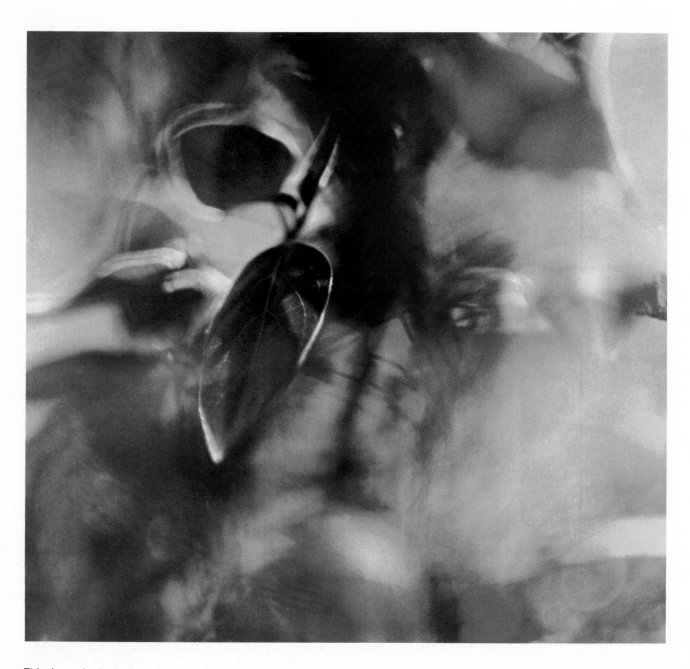

This is a single leaf of Japanese honeysuckle in its own private jungle. Reality is only suggested by the use of selective focus, but the colors and other forms still bring out the full environment of the leaf.

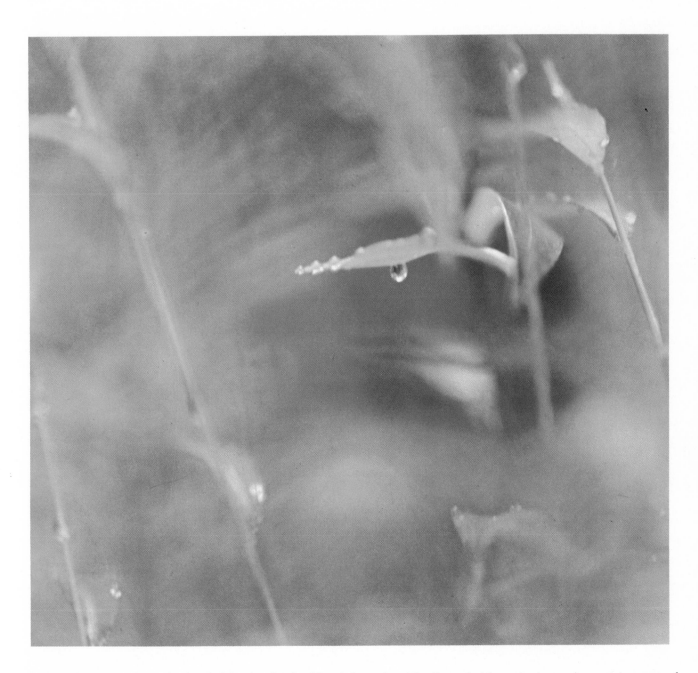

A tiny raindrop becomes the jeweled focal point in this photograph, while the out-of-focus background suggests some of the mystery of nature itself. Sunlight through a dead oak leaf provides the touch of red behind the raindrop.

Abstracts

Overleaf: (Page 12) A collection of assorted international rocks. (Photo by Ray Simons) (Page 13) Seven-year-old chimpanzee. (Photo courtesy of Wild Acres Zoo, Largo, Florida)

Spring Flowers

by Anne D. Murphy

Photography by Jerome Drown

Alive, awakened from winter's bed, through mother earth's warming bosom they've sprung. To recall those memories—blurred by days of November's gray and brown—they dress in gowns of rainbow hue to herald the coming of their season, the spring.

Spring Flowers

first snow and beech leaves Photo by Ray Simons

Florida Sunset
Photo by Gerald Irish

Animals have the right of way

By John J. Chalmers
Photography by the Author

A black-maned adult male lion, the king of the beasts, overlooks his domain.

This sleek cheetah, world's fastest animal, has just run down a small Thomson's gazelle and is beginning a late afternoon feast.

An extremely long tail is characteristic of the vervet monkey.

Kongoni, or hartebeests, have horns which resemble bicycle handlebars.

Kenya is now an independent member of the Commonwealth, but the British left their mark on this former colony in East Africa in many ways. For one thing, cars in Kenya all drive on the "wrong" side of the road. But there is one traffic regulation which the British never wrote: Animals have the right of way.

In Kenya's many game reserves and parks, the motorist will have to yield to the abundant wildlife that knows nothing of British colonization, African independence or traffic laws. However, few drivers are going to argue if a lumbering elephant crosses the road, or a curious young impala blocks traffic, or if a baboon leaps on the hood of a car that has stopped to allow its passengers a better look at a family of warthogs.

The wildlife of Kenya is a prime tourist attraction; and the capital city, Nairobi, is a popular place for visitors. Although hunting licenses are expensive for the nonresident who wants to collect his own trophies, it costs only the price of film to shoot with a camera; and Kenya offers unlimited targets of wild game in natural environments.

Only five miles from downtown Nairobi is Nairobi National Park, a game reserve that contains hundreds of species of animals and birds that can be seen at close range in a couple of hours' drive through the park. Ranging in size from the tiny deerlike dik-dik to the tanklike hippopotamus, and from weaverbirds to ostriches, the game provides a sight-seeing thrill found only in Africa.

Few subjects make a better shot through a telephoto lens than a sleek cheetah with a fresh kill, a princely leopard watching the grassland from his branch in a

18

The large wildebeest, dark gray with darker stripes on its forequarters, can be seen alone or in groups.

The wide-striped Burchell's zebra is a common sight.

tree, or the rhythmic running grace of a towering giraffe.

Although there are no elephants in Nairobi Park itself, they are not far away, and the visitor can travel to several places to see them. For example, a 150-mile safari south of Nairobi leads to the Masai Amboseli Game Reserve, a huge game sanctuary in southern Kenya, bordering on Tanzania. To reach Amboseli, the traveler goes on dusty dirt and gravel roads across the endless stretches of brown grassland that undulate in rolling waves from horizon to horizon, dotted occasionally by scrubby whistling thorn trees.

Frequently seen are grazing herds of zebra and hartebeest or a lone wildebeest. Not uncommon in these lands

The mighty big-horned African buffalo will weigh up to 2,000 pounds when fullgrown. In the background above the clouds is the top of Mount Kilimanjaro, an ever-present sight at Amboseli Game Reserve.

19

Wild elephants group together as they roam the Amboseli Game Reserve.

are ostriches, and it's easy to spot the male as his long periscope neck extends straight up from a giant ball of black and white feathers.

Farther on, the land becomes decorated with large hills, and greener with numerous shrubs and bushes. Here grows the V-shaped, flat-topped, yellow-barked acacia thorn tree so common in Kenya. Its upper branches provide food for the giraffe, which stretches to eat off the very top of the tree. Also common here are the huge anthills of hard red earth, sometimes eight feet high.

This is all Masai country, home of the primitive and colorful Masai tribe, famed for their prowess as hunters of *simba*, the lion. They hunt the lion armed with buffalo-skin shields and long, steel-bladed spears, which they hurl like javelins. The *manyattas*, or villages, where these warriors live in small brown pincushion cow-dung-and-mud huts can be seen along the road among the trees.

At Amboseli the visitor can stay in a modern lodge, a tent or a thatched-roof banda, where he sleeps under a mosquito net; but at least here he has the advantage of an incongruous modern bathroom. Game is abundant at the Amboseli Reserve, and for only $1.50 a day a park ranger will accompany the sightseers and lead them to the animals. It's a little money well spent when the ranger takes you to watch a dozen great gray ivory-tusked elephants graze a hundred feet away.

An amazing thing about these giants of the forest is the way they move almost silently through the brush. When grazing, they are also quiet except for a bit of chomping noise, or an occasional loud crack when a muscular trunk snakes out to snap off the branch of a tree.

Besides the elephant, the powerful African buffalo, the lordly lion, the squinty-eyed rhino and other game at Amboseli, there is another unforgettable sight. Across the border in Tanzania looms the magnificent Mount Kilimanjaro, one of the most splendid mountains creation ever built. Rising from the plains at 3,500 feet above sea level, "Killy" reaches its height of 19,500 feet at Kibo Peak with its snow-covered flat top

surveying Africa in timeless grandeur three and a half miles above the surrounding land.

Other interesting trips are available. A hundred miles northwest of Nairobi (on a paved road this time) is the pleasant city of Nakuru, with nearby Menengai Crater, a great extinct volcanic bowl with a rim 7,500 feet above sea level, and a floor which is now covered with 35 square miles of forest. Also nearby is Nakuru Bird Sanctuary, where thousands of pink flamingos line the shores of Lake Nakuru.

The way to Nakuru leads past plains and hills, and over the escarpment into the gigantic Rift Valley, a thousand feet deep and ranging from thirty-five to a hundred miles across. Stretching from north to south, the valley's size is so great that it is best seen from the air, and if the pilot doesn't point it out to incoming visitors, it can hardly be missed.

North of Nairobi, the road leads through greener country to the well-known Outspan Hotel, where a splendid five-course dinner costs only $1.75. The Outspan is the departure point for the famous Treetops Hotel, the unique rustic building where Princess Elizabeth stayed one night in February, 1952, and awoke to the news that George VI had died, and she was now Queen Elizabeth II.

It was at the Outspan where Lord Baden-Powell, founder of the Boy Scouts, spent his last days and died in one of the cabins. He is buried nearby, as he requested, in a small cemetery where his grave has an uninterrupted view of rugged Mount Kenya, whose highest rocky peak is over 17,000 feet high.

In Nairobi fantastic blooms of bougainvillea, hibiscus, sweet-scented frangipani, purple jacaranda tree blossoms and tall tousle-headed palms decorate the city's streets. Nairobi, located at 5,500 feet above sea level and 90 miles south of the equator, is bright and busy with many modern new structures such as office buildings, hotels, the university and Parliament buildings.

The craft shops alone prove a great attraction for tourists who want to buy handmade wooden carvings created by a native tribesman, or exotic skin products made from the hides of a wild animal. Such items are popular not only with the tourists. In Kenya there are many Canadians, Americans and Englishmen living and working; and they, too, patronize the local craftsmen.

Summer in Kenya begins in December, and for four months before the rains begin, the country offers perfect weather for visitors—clear air, high temperatures and sapphire skies. Indeed Nairobi rightfully calls herself "The City in the Sun."

The red wolf (although he isn't actually red in color) is almost extinct. Only about 300 remain in the United States. Photo by Hal Swiggett, courtesy of the Department of the Interior.

Saga of the WOLF

By Norman B. Wiltsey

The wolf's fate is not yet irrevocably sealed; his destiny still hangs in the balance of public opinion

When animals of all kinds were plentiful in North America and only the Indian and Eskimo were present to take toll of nature's bounty, wolves ranged in large numbers across the country from coast to coast and from mid-Mexico to the Arctic tundra.

The Indian hunter, an instinctive conservationist, had a deep, mystical regard for the wolf and rarely killed one unless his need for food

and hides was great. The inland Eskimo hunted wolves only to make garments of their fur.

Unfortunately, the wolf was held in no such esteem by the newly arrived colonists. The species had always lived in rhythmic equilibrium with other species until the arrival of the first colonists from Europe upset nature's dynamic ecological balance. All-out war was declared upon the wolf, and clearing off the primeval forests of the East was the initial blow. As the great trees fell under the busy saws and axes of the pioneers and the thin, irregular line of the frontier pushed westward, the wolves retreated into the Great Plains and the mountains of the western wilderness.

Today, nearly 400 years after the North American wolf began his struggle for survival against encroaching man, the species has continued to dwindle in numbers. Scientists, who have studied the total disappearance of bird and animal species, claim the wolf population is "critical"—a level below which a species suddenly becomes extinct.

Canis lupus, the gray or timber wolf, is considerably more numerous than the red wolf, *Canis rufus*. Our largest remaining group of timber wolves ranges in the North Woods of Michigan, Wisconsin and Minnesota. It is significant that this beautiful, still unspoiled wilderness area also contains the largest and hardiest deer herd in America, as it is one of the few forest regions where the wolf is permitted to carry out his role in nature's plan to preserve only the fittest of a species. The old, the sick and the weak deer fall prey to the wolf; only the healthy and strong animals survive to procreate their kind.

As it is with the deer, so it is with the caribou of Alaska and the Arctic tundra, where the wolf culls the herds of weaklings. Eskimo legend says that the caribou and the wolf care for each other, for the caribou feeds the wolf, but the wolf keeps the caribou strong.

Big-game hunters have long maintained that the wolf takes enormous toll of deer and caribou and must, therefore, be exterminated as a ruthless predator. Actually, as biologists have determined through field observation and documented in numerous reports, the wolf is a natural controlling factor necessary to the continued welfare of all three species. Curiously, many experienced hunters are either ignorant of or oblivious to the wolf's primary function in fauna preservation. Others, perhaps better informed but still prejudiced against the wolf, scoff at the careful scientific findings of qualified observers.

Hunting magazines furnish ammunition for the stubbornly antiwolf faction with inflammatory articles, even occasionally dragging out the hoary tale that wolves frequently go on a meat drunk, killing many more animals than required to satisfy their hunger. Actually, like all predators, the wolf kills only when hungry himself or to feed his family.

In 40 years of wildlife observation, I have found evidence of only one such multiple kill. One hard winter of much snow, intense cold and widespread starvation in the Canadian forest of northern Ontario, I came upon the skeletons of five deer which almost certainly had been killed by wolves. The deer had "yarded up" after a heavy snowfall and, unable to escape through the surrounding deep snow, had fallen easy prey to the gaunt gray hunters.

My Indian guide assured me that such a kill occurred only when the wolves were actually starving, and that at such a time all lupine property rights were dispensed with and that all wolves within calling range were invited to share in the kill.

Like all carnivorous animals, the wolf has an enormous appetite. By actual test, an adult wolf has been known to eat almost one fifth of his own weight at a single meal. It is also true that the adult male wolf has to hunt throughout the night and often far into the day to provide food for his mate and her pups from the time the youngsters stop nursing at about three weeks until they can be trained to hunt for themselves at eight to ten weeks. If the hunt produces no more than a rabbit, most of the meat is brought back to the home den and the male starts again on his endless rounds. The male wolf is an attentive husband (the wolf mates for life) and a devoted parent. He never shirks his fatherly role of provider for his family.

As a wolf's hunting range may extend over 10 to 20 miles, the nightly search for food entails not only sacrifice but hard work. When a kill is made a long distance from the den, the male will eat heavily of the meat, then return to his family and regurgitate it for his mate and her pups to feed upon. Litters of from four to eight pups are not uncommon, giving the male a tremendous feeding task. Often the assistance of another adult male in the clan will be enlisted to help support the voracious little newcomers.

On the Arctic tundra, mice form the major summer diet of the wolf. Tundra wolves are also accomplished fishermen, catching Arctic sculpins, suckers and even the great Northern pike or jackfish when at spawning time in the spring these big fish invade the marshes along the lakeshores. In each case the wolf varies his fishing technique to fit conditions and quarry.

Sculpin are small fish which lurk under rocks in shoal water, and the wolf catches these simply by wading along the shore, turning over the rocks

WOLF

with paws or nose and snapping up the sculpin before it can get away.

For catching suckers, the wolf emulates the salmon-catching method of the bear, posting himself on a rock in a shallow section of the stream and scooping up the fish as they pass on their spawning runs.

The pike, sometimes weighing up to 35 or 40 pounds, present a greater challenge. In this instance, the wolf will wade upstream, driving the pike ahead of him until the fish is hopelessly trapped in a narrow, shallow channel.

Most pups are whelped in April or May. They are fuzzy little fellows and are gray, brownish gray or blackish in color. Their growth is rapid. In less than a year they are practically as large as their parents, ranging up to 24 inches high at the shoulder and weighing up to 100 pounds. The Arctic wolf may reach a weight of 170 pounds. In all cases, the female is about 20 percent smaller than the male. In color the adult timber wolf ranges from dark gray to silver gray, grayish brown, reddish brown, grayish white or even black. White wolves are common in the Arctic, a protective color that fits their winter environment. Magnificent cream-colored pelts have been taken in Alaska and in the Canadian Northwest Territories.

Cattlemen are just as vehement as big-game hunters in their denunciation of the wolf as an insatiable predator. "Wolves have no place in livestock areas," stated South Dakota ranch owner Jim Moran in a recent letter to the author. "With the help of the government hunters, we've finally got 'em killed off in ranch country, and we don't want to see them come sneaking back. Wolves belong in wilderness country."

Biologists and naturalists agree with the cattlemen that wolves cannot be permitted to range in ranch country, and heartily concur in the logical belief that wolves belong in wilderness areas. Naturalist Stanley P. Young wrote in a past issue of *American Forests*, "Where not in conflict with human interests, wolves may well be left alone. They form one of the most interesting groups of all mammals and should be permitted to have a place in North American fauna."

Government biologist Adolph Murie echoed Young's sentiments in his book *The Wolves of Mount McKinley*: "Many feel that our national parks and monuments are fitting places for just such a purpose (wolf sanctuary). Congress has set aside these areas to preserve, among other things, the native fauna. Mount McKinley National Park is the only national park in which wolves occur in numbers."

Upon conclusion of his study of the wolf and the general ecological picture in Mount McKinley National Park, Murie stated, "First it seems apparent that the wolf is the chief check on the increase of the dall sheep in Mount McKinley Park. . . . Furthermore, it was found that the sheep preyed upon, other than lambs, were generally old or diseased and therefore already doomed to an early death. . . . The caribou is the main food of the wolves, and a heavy toll of the calves is taken. Yet the park herd of between 20,000 and 30,000 animals is apparently maintaining its numbers."

More than any other wild animal in history, the wolf has suffered from a bad press. He has been branded a "man killer—a ravening, savage beast." Yet, refuting the oft-repeated charge that the wolf is a man killer if given the slightest opportunity, U.S. Fish and Wildlife scientists state unequivocally that a half century of painstaking investigation has disclosed only a handful of instances of a wolf attacking a man. Yearly statistics reveal that human beings are killed by bulls, wild dogs—often erroneously called wolves—snakes, spiders, wasps and bees. No death has ever been listed as due to a wolf or so-called "wolf pack." (Wolves often travel together in family groups of from four or five to a dozen, hence the lurid tales of fierce "wolf packs" that crop up periodically in the newspapers.)

As for Canadian statistics on the matter of killer wolves, the distinguished author-biologist Farley Mowat writes in his book *Never Cry Wolf*: "There is no record of wolves ever having killed a human being in the Canadian North; although there must have been times when the temptation was well-nigh irresistible."

The fate of the wolf is not yet irrevocably sealed; his destiny still hangs in the balance of public opinion. He may yet survive. If he does not, man, the great destroyer, will have erased forever another strand in nature's living pattern.

And all persons who, like myself, have been privileged to hear the feral song of the hunting wolf on a frosty wilderness midnight will feel a sense of irreparable loss.

These grizzly cubs will
remain with their mothers
until they are
about two years old.

GRIZZLIES:

Marvel of Nature or Menace to Man?

By Bill Thomas

Without our help, another species could become history

They call him king of the North American wilderness, but since there's little wilderness left and since it is a diminishing quality, the grizzly bear is, in effect, an endangered species. Its depletion will mark but another creature to join a growing list of life forms passing into history.

In recent years, too much public demand has been not upon saving this king of the forest but upon destroying it. Its conflict with man, who keeps pushing the inroads of civilization farther and farther into the few brief wilderness frontiers, has on occasion led to violence and death. And all too often, the blame has been improperly placed upon the grizzly, not upon mankind where many naturalists claim it rightfully belongs.

The grizzly is powerful and legendary. He has been depicted by artists and writers as some sort of hairy, bloodthirsty devil of the wilds. And because of this combination, because of the fearful stories told down through the genera-

Photo by John and Frank Craighead

25

This portrait of a grizzly shows his massive head, small ears and small eyes.

tions about him, man took little trouble to learn something of his nature, his ecology, his character and his needs. Instead, he was something to be avoided, or barring that, killed. For years he has been hunted as a challenging sport by too many men who saw nothing in the grizzly but a bearskin rug.

Not too many years ago, the grizzly population in the lower 48 states alone numbered in the thousands. Today, it is not expected to exceed 700. And yet two states—Montana and Alaska—still have hunting seasons on grizzly. The number of grizzly bears killed in Alaska annually outnumbers the total population of the lower 48 states. In 1966, for instance, 856 grizzly bear kills were tabulated in the 49th state.

While it's true that Alaska has far more grizzlies than any other state—in fact more than all the lower 48 states combined—grizzlies undoubtedly will become more and more rare there, too, as industry and man suppress their domain.

The grizzly went largely unnoticed by the general public until the summer of 1967. In one night two separate episodes in Glacier National Park near the Canadian border of Montana brought the grizzly into the headlines, and the pressures that followed were strongly in favor of annihilating the big bears. Two young college girls, in separate incidents by separate bears, were maimed and killed.

The girls—Julie Helgeson, 19, of the University of Minnesota, and Michele Koons, 19, of California Western University—were on wilderness hiking-camping jaunts when the attacks came during an August night. Both were summer employees at the park, and both were accompanied by one or more persons on the hike. Both were fatally mauled and bitten while in their sleeping bags.

These two confrontations of man by grizzlies were not the first nor the last. But they were unique because of their similarities and because they have never been fully explained. Naturalists, park officials and other investigators have pointed out a number of things that could have provoked the attacks, however, including a garbage dump nearby in Julie Helgeson's case and littering over a period of months by fishermen and other campers nearby in the case of Michele Koons.

The bears naturally had become hooked on the habit of feeding on the garbage and since, naturalists believe, the grizzly considers his feeding ground his own private domain, he resents intruders. This could have been a large factor in both cases.

Secondly, the bear at Trout Lake which killed Michele Koons was accustomed to opening backpacks to procure morsels of food within them. He may have thought the sleeping bag in which the girl slept was merely another package of food; and when she screamed and struggled to get away, the bear was infuriated and increased the intensity of the attack.

It was discovered that one of the bears had cubs nearby, and that could certainly have been a contributing factor, too.

Both bears were shot by park rangers, and the public decried blame upon the grizzly. But blame could well have been placed elsewhere—upon the fishermen and other campers who littered the area with food, drawing bears into the area over a period of months, causing them to make this a regular prowling and feeding ground, and upon the officials of the U.S. Park Service, who allowed an open dump to be operated just behind a wilderness chalet, primarily, it would seem, for the purpose of drawing bears for the guests to watch.

Not so long ago grizzlies were almost never seen by visitors to national parks except on remote trails into the back country. Even then, unless there were extenuating circumstances, the grizzly, if given the chance, would turn tail and run rather than attack. Under normal conditions he will do so today.

But things are changing. Man's push into the wilderness, and thus into the grizzly's domain, is bringing about a difference in the animal's behavior. He is becoming more conditioned to having people around, but his temperament is not such that he can be trusted or his actions predicted. During the summer of 1969, I watched two mature grizzlies cavort playfully within a hundred yards of one of the principal thoroughfares of Yellowstone National Park. And I watched also as car after car stopped while men, women and children crowded on foot to within 25 or 30 yards of these bears to photograph or call out to them.

To many park visitors a bear is a bear and these were no different from the black ones that had greeted them at the roadside as they entered the park. They were no different from those that fed from the hand. On occasion, I was told by a park ranger, bears have been stoned by children who knew no better, a factor certainly serious enough to provoke an attack.

Another grizzly was making nightly visits to the campground where I camped near the south entrance, a good 25 miles away. And yet, three years previously when I visited the park in August, I was told that grizzlies almost never visited a campground; it was against their very nature to linger in areas where there were many people.

The laws of nature that apply to other wild life—indeed to man himself—in the most basic form also apply to the grizzly. While it is possible to find exceptions to almost any situation, generally speaking, a grizzly will seldom attack unless he is provoked in some way. If you corner him, he will attack. If you persist in trailing him or lingering in what he considers his domain, he may charge. If you get between a sow bear and her cubs, you can expect trouble. You could expect the same thing from almost any form of wildlife. If you get within a few yards of a blue jay's nest, the bird will often dive at your head or flog you with its wings. But if you avoid the domain, if you treat an animal fairly, it will avoid you. Even a rattlesnake, if given an opportunity to retreat, will do so rather than strike.

Grizzlies can be vicious, as evidenced by the attacks on the two girls in Glacier National Park, but they can also be lovable. They are intelligent, can outrun a racehorse, are strong enough to bash in an automobile door with one swipe of the paw, have a very good memory and more reasoning power than any other wild animal, including the chimpanzee.

Dr. William T. Hornaday, former director of the Bronx Zoo, gave specially prepared tests to a number of animals in a research project a few years back and found that on reasoning power the grizzly rated a score of 100 percent, while the chimp rated only 75 percent. Naturalist Ernest Thompson Seton wrote, "Wise grizzlies and superwise there always were, and mediocre and fools. But the fools went early; they were weeded out by the hunters as soon as repeating rifles appeared. The stupid and the commonplace went next, and the ten-times sifted remnant are the wisest of the wise in their kind."

An example of their unusual intelligence is borne out by the documented story of two grizzly cubs found by one Enos A. Mills, who took them to his cabin. Within 24 hours, Mills wrote, they each knew their new names and responded to them.

Naturalist-author W. J. Schoonmaker

states in
his book *The
World of the Grizzly
Bear* a belief that bears as well as
other wild animals have a sixth sense
which enables them to know whether
or not a person means to harm them.
He believes this may have prompted
some grizzly attacks in the past
upon individuals carrying guns or
other weapons into areas occupied
by grizzlies.

Seton, incidentally, believed the
grizzly can be fully domesticated,
whereas the black bear, according
to his statements, can never be fully
tamed. As early as 1860, actress
Lola Montez kept two full-grown
grizzly pets chained to the front of her
cottage in Grass Valley, California.

Perhaps the most famous tame
grizzly stories are of those owned
by Grizzly Adams, a California
hunter, who trained two bears
to be his constant hunting

The winter coat of the grizzly bear is
composed of thick fleecy underfur
with projecting long guard hairs.

Photo by W. J. Schoonmaker   29

companions. One of these, Lady Washington, was taught to be a regular pack animal and with a saddle would carry loads up to 200 pounds. Another of Adams' grizzlies was Ben Franklin, who assisted Adams in hunting.

In order to show the docility of his bears, Adams would unchain Ben Franklin and ride on his back. In the summer of 1860, Adams and his bears performed in P. T. Barnum's show in New York City, a highlight in their career. On opening day he paraded his animals down Broadway and through the Bowery. Three rode in a wagon with him, and only two were chained. The third bear, General Fremont, was unchained, and Adams periodically rode on his back.

Once tamed, they were docile and loving, but they certainly took their toll while being trained, for later that same year Adams died of injuries sustained over the years as the result of training his grizzlies. One had nearly scalped him once; others had given him numerous head injuries, which ultimately led to his death.

One naturalist who knew personally of several tamed grizzlies during his experience described the tame grizzly as possessing "that gentle, flawless kind of character that we look for in a dog." But he added that an adult grizzly cannot be tamed.

A Colorado rancher who raised two grizzly cubs tells the story of their cunningness and speed. The cubs were allowed to come and go around the ranch as they pleased. At the end of four years, one of them died from poison. The other, because he resented being teased by a neighboring rancher who visited frequently, was taken many miles from the ranch by the keeper and released. The big bear was back at the ranch eight hours before the return of the man who released him.

At Yellowstone Park in 1968 a grizzly that had been visiting a campground frequently was trapped and transported 25 miles to a site in the adjoining Gallatin National Forest and released. That bear did not miss a visit, for he was back that same evening to go through the camp garbage cans again.

The grizzly is indeed a noble animal. Its pan-shaped face, its kind eyes, the silver tips of its fur, the hump on its shoulders, belie the vicious character with which it has been labeled. At one time the grizzly ranged throughout the northwestern and western United States. But grizzlies were natural enemies to man's endeavors from the outset. They destroyed cattle and sheep and thus were unpopular with ranchers. Bounties were offered in the middle 1800's in almost every western state. Furs were in demand and brought $10 each in days when the dollar really meant something.

Thus the grizzly population began to diminish. And it has never stopped. The last-known grizzly in northern California was killed in 1902; and none have been found in other parts of that state since 1922. The last two were reported in Oregon in 1894; no grizzly has been known in Texas since 1890. In 1952, the U.S. Fish and Wildlife Service census reported a total grizzly population in the lower 48 states of 1,208 bears. And just seven years later that number dropped to 856, representing a decrease of approximately one fourth.

The greatest known concentrations of grizzlies anywhere are at two locations—on Admiralty Island near Juneau, Alaska, and in Yellowstone National Park. It isn't really known how many grizzlies live on Admiralty Island, but an estimated 250 inhabit Yellowstone. They are protected, of course, and, according to a U.S. Fish and Wildlife Service official, are "holding their own." Montana wildlife officials believe the grizzly is holding his own there, too, in spite of hunting permits.

But the general picture is indeed grim. The grizzly bear is no less important than the whooping crane. And while our last-minute efforts have rallied the kind of support to gingerly protect the whooping crane, it will undoubtedly be more difficult to gain that kind of ground for the grizzly. But regardless of his nature, regardless of the picture so imprinted upon our minds of his vicious character, that kind of support and care must be forthcoming. Otherwise, the grizzly, like so many other species of life upon earth, will live only in legend. And that indeed would be an unpardonable sin.

Photographing Desert Royalty

By H. Wayland Barrows

Photography by the Author

"Easy does it, just step to one side a bit, now turn just a bit this way. That's fine. Just one more pose, O.K., now look this way—." These could be directions to a nervous bride, a glamorous model, a man of distinction or any of a dozen subjects willing to pose for my camera. This time, however, it was different; I was photographing royalty. My subject was the king of the desert crags himself, the majestic bighorn ram.

For years I had planned and waited for this moment, but never in my most colorful dreams had I hoped to find such a cooperative model. And I found myself giving gentle instructions as I would to a human model, as if this majestic creature could understand me.

The time was early August. The place was the biological research area in that fantastic piece of southern California desert real estate known as Joshua Tree National Monument.

Months earlier I had obtained a permit to allow my brother Frank and me to enter the area. Our goal was to locate and photograph the phantom desert sheep that were rumored to be out there.

Photographing
Desert Royalty

Now the day had arrived, and I was going alone. Urgent business delayed Frank, but he planned to join me later.

It was nearly noon when I parked the Scout and shouldered my pack basket which contained my camera equipment, a light lunch and a plastic gallon jug of water. It was a beautiful day. The sun was bright and the sky a turquoise blue with cotton white clouds. My little thermometer read a comfortable 85° F. The trail was easy to follow; and a half hour after leaving the Scout, I was climbing the hill that overlooked that spot where a tiny trickle of water calls all surrounding wildlife.

The half hour hike was quiet; no wild creature made its presence known, and most of the way my footsteps were in sand. As I climbed the hill, I became aware of the soft call of the mountain quail, and occasionally I caught glimpses of them as they scurried through the sage and mesquite.

At the top of the hill, I paused for a close, deliberate survey of the area. A slow turn to the left nearly caused me to fall out of the straps of my pack basket, for there, about 50 feet away, stood a sleek mature ewe. She calmly watched me as we stared at each other for a moment; and then, as she didn't seem in a hurry to leave, I suddenly remembered that I was there to take pictures. Knowing that quick movements tend to frighten wild animals, I tried to be especially careful while setting up my tripod and mounting my Bolex.

A quick meter reading showed the correct lens adjustment, and then, to set the scene, I ran off a few feet of film using the normal 12mm.

lens. Then I quickly swung the turret around to the 36mm. lens for some frame-filling closeups. Until now, I had seen only the one sheep, but I knew there might be others that I hadn't spotted. I looked around intently without seeing another sheep, but what was that suspicious curl behind that bush over there? I dug into the pack basket once more and focused my seven-power glass on the spot. The curl I had seen was the horn of a mature ram and close beside him was another fine ewe.

Things were getting more interesting by the minute! This last pair were not in a good spot for photographing, but I decided to hold my position. Maybe Frank would come in time to see them too. A flat rock nearby seemed inviting.

I had been seated on the rock only a few minutes when the sound of a stone being dislodged on the opposite hillside caught my ear. There must be more sheep coming. Sure enough, around the bend on a trail came two more ewes followed by another handsome ram. They weren't in a hurry, but one of the ewes came directly down to the waterhole. When she moved in, 50 or more quail scattered, each one verbally objecting to the intruder. The ewe didn't seem to notice them. In the meantime, the ram and the second ewe had gone directly to the pair which were lying screened by the bushes. This pair got up to meet them, and soon they were all out in the open.

What a sight! Two mature rams with full curl horns escorted by two beautiful ewes, slick as seals and apparently in the best of health. All this I was trying to record on movie film. The sheep were aware of my presence but were apparently ignoring me. The only times they seemed to take notice was when I moved the tripod to a different location to obtain shots from a different angle.

I was glad to get the movies but wanted some good stills, too. Now might be a good time to see what could be done with my Rollie.

Moving along a little game trail which ran across the face of the hill, I began to quietly talk to the sheep. From experience as a farmer, I knew that animals don't understand what you say to them, but that they nearly always understand your tone of voice; and these sheep were no exception. They began to show trust and curiosity that had not been evident before. One of the ewes daintily picked her way across the valley and came up the trail to within a few feet of me. She cocked her head to one side and looked at me as if to say, "What is it that you really want?" Of course, it was that pose—and

Photographing
Desert Royalty

I quickly snapped what turned out to be one of my best pictures.

I don't know what she told her friends when she went back, but soon one of the rams was coming my way by an indirect route. I got one shot of him peeking at me from behind a bush. He kept coming and I kept shooting, climaxing the whole show when he climbed up onto a huge boulder about 30 feet away, giving me a grand silhouette shot with the blue sky as a background. These were the moments I described in the opening paragraph of this story. This was a nature photographer's dream come true.

Film was running low by this time, and I arrived back just in time to meet Frank. "Sorry to be late," he began, "but I just had to stop and take a sheep picture." Then he went on to describe how a fine ewe and ram had crossed the trail ahead of him, and how he had followed them and had finally succeeded in getting some good shots. Was he being just a bit smug?

When I led him to see "my sheep," he just stood there in amazement. We counted an even dozen. As we watched them, his ram and ewe joined the little flock. This enlarged the group to 14. Five mature rams, eight ewes and one lamb. We wondered about this ratio and why only one lamb. These sheep appeared healthy and well fed. Was it predators? There surely were abundant coyote signs in evidence. On a previous trip to this area I had seen one of the largest bobcats I had ever seen running wild. This was a possible answer, although not necessarily the right one.

It didn't take Frank long to get his cameras organized. I enjoyed a grandstand seat as I watched him work with his Contarex and Linhof. He is a semipro who got his start as a combat photographer in World War II; and now, among his other duties, he is an instructor in photography at the La Sierra campus of Loma Linda University in California. It was fascinating to watch him as he collected black-and-white shots with one camera and then reached out for color with the other. Almost before we knew it, it was time to leave. Our permit said we were to be out of the area by 6 o'clock. With reluctance we packed our gear for the trip out. What a day it had been!

We spoke once again to the sheep, "Good-bye, friends, and may your tribe increase."

34

HAVE YOU SEEN A TULE ELK?

By Joe Van Wormer

If you haven't, you may have to hurry. The tule elk is high on the Department of the Interior's list of rare and endangered mammals. The latest count indicates that fewer than 300 of them may now be in existence.

When Europeans first began colonizing along the Atlantic Coast, there were three species and three subspecies of elk on the continent. Two of these, the Eastern or Canadian elk (*Cervus canadensis canadensis* Erxleben) and the Merriam elk (*Cervus merriami* Nelson), were killed off by settlers by 1900.

The tule elk (*Cervus nannodes* Merriam) did not fare well either; and it's only by the grace of God and Henry Miller that this species did not

35

ELK

This newly born tule elk calf shows the protective coloration which helps him to blend with his surroundings. Elk cows usually bear one calf in late April or May. Occasionally twins are born.

disappear in 1873. According to some reports, only one pair was left at that time. If this is true, today's entire population of tule elk descended from that one pair of survivors. Henry Miller, of the Miller and Lux Company, a large ranch in Kern County, California, upon whose land the remnants of the tule elk lived, ordered his cowhands not to molest the elk and to protect them from hunters. It is remarkable that the species survived at all after being reduced to the absolute minimum needed for existence, but survive they did.

The tule elk problem continues to exist, however, and in the nearly 100 years since Henry Miller decided tule elk were worth saving, little has been accomplished toward an adequate solution to their plight.

As late as the 1800's, the great San Joaquin and Sacramento valleys of California still had large populations of elk, deer and pronghorn. One resident of that period described the animals as being present in such numbers "that they actually darkened the plains for miles, and looked in the distance like great herds of cattle."

The range of tule elk at that time extended from Butte County, 80 miles north of Sacramento, south to the Buena Vista Lake region near Bakersfield in Kern County, and from the western slope of the Sierras to the coast ranges.

Though early California explorers lived off the land and killed many tule elk, their take probably had little effect on the total elk population. But as more and more settlers arrived, the elk herds began to show the effect as hunters increased their kill to meet the demands for fresh meat in this fast-growing area. The Gold Rush brought in thousands of gold-hungry miners, who were too busy digging to provide for themselves and relied upon market hunters to supply them with meat. Much of it was tule elk meat.

The rich valleys were envied by eager ranchers, who considered elk as competitors with their livestock in the natural grazing areas—and trespassers when they foraged on cultivated crops. The ranchers encouraged the destruction of the elk, as did the Elk Lodge brothers who fancied elks' teeth watch fobs as symbols of their membership. By the 1870's the last of thousands of tule elk were hiding in the tule (bulrush) marshes north of Buena Vista Lake. It was this that apparently brought them their name of "tule elk" and the erroneous reputation of being marsh dwellers. Their natural habitat is the open grass valley. Even their retreat into this forbidding marsh country brought no relief, for unrelenting hunters took after them in boats, from which lookouts searched out the animals from ladders lashed to the masts.

It is fortunate that the last of the tule elk happened to be where Henry Miller could do something about them. The herd increased on the Miller and Lux Company ranch, although it was some 30 years before it became large enough to create much interest. Some transplant operations were attempted in 1904 and 1905 but with little success. By 1914 the Miller and Lux herd had grown to an estimated 400 and were doing approximately $7,000 worth of damage each year to alfalfa fields and fences.

More transplants were tried with varying degrees of success; but, in general, the newly established populations did not prosper and eventually died out. For a while both Yosemite National Park and Sequoia National Park had tule elk in exhibition pastures, but a subsequent national park policy against exhibiting caged animals or nonnative animals eliminated these small herds.

A 900-acre fenced reserve was created in 1932 at Tupman, a few miles from Bakersfield. Although this is the tule elk's natural habitat, the limited space of the reserve does not permit them to exist under anything like natural conditions. The herd is presently maintained at between 30 and 40 animals. They are fed on artificial feeds as the area is not large enough to provide the needed amounts of natural food.

In 1933 and 1934 transplants were made to Owens Valley, located between Kings Canyon National Park and Sequoia National Park on the west and the Inyo Mountains on the east. The valley is about 50 miles long and 10 miles wide. Most of the land is owned by the city of Los Angeles, which bought it originally to obtain water rights to the Owens River and its tributaries. It then leased some of the land back to ranchers, who use it to graze livestock and grow such crops as corn, potatoes and alfalfa.

Although Owens Valley is much higher and

drier than their former low-country home, the transplanted tule elk did well and multiplied. Soon they were in trouble with the area's ranchers. A hungry elk is no respector of fences or property rights. Complaints of elk damages produced results in the form of controlled hunts for the purpose of keeping the population between 250 and 300 animals, a number it is presumed someone determined the valley could support without excessive crop damages resulting.

In March, 1967, the Los Angeles City Council adopted a resolution that would "authorize that portion of Owens Valley land lying between Tinemah and Owens Lake to be set aside as a wildlife refuge."

Two years later nothing has yet been done to implement this authorized refuge, and it must be assumed that opponents of the idea have been able to forestall the establishment of the refuge.

I made a recent trip to Owens Valley just to get a look at the tule elk. I spent three days traveling from dawn to dusk over dusty back roads as well as paved highways, and scoured the area thoroughly with binoculars. Despite verbal assistance from the California Department of Fish and Game office in Bishop, I saw only ten tule elk. One herd of seven cows was taking

Above: Two young bull elk sparring.

Photo by Leonard Lee Rue III

Right: An adult bull elk may weigh up to 700 pounds, considerably less than other elk.

Photo by Leonard Lee Rue III

Photo by Gerhard Bakker from the Committee for the Preservation of the Tule Elk

This herd of tule elk is found at Owens Valley, California, where the population is maintained at just under 300 animals.

ELK

it easy on the side of a sage-covered knoll near U.S. Highway 395, and a group of three ran across a rocky slope several miles west of the highway. The group of seven were extremely nervous; and when I stopped the car for a better look, they left in a hurry. This lack of sociability was undoubtedly the result of harassment from ranchers in the area.

Still wanting a good look at one of these animals, I drove over the Tupman Reserve. The herd of 35 head had segregated themselves into a bull herd and a cow herd, although the latter had some immature bulls included. They could be studied easily from the visitor's area with the aid of binoculars; and at times, I was told, they graze or feed within a few yards of their inter-ested audience. They were, I suspect, in good condition for confined animals. However, I would have preferred to see them in natural-looking terrain. It certainly seemed to me that we should have done better by one of the rarest animals in the world during the past 100 years. Even the bison has fared better. There are probably more bison on the National Bison Range in Montana than there are tule elk in existence.

Maybe a refuge in Owens Valley is the answer, although refuges require proper management to be effective. I can sympathize with the ranchers in the valley whose livestock operations might be jeopardized by the creation of such a refuge. However, there are a lot of pasturelands in the world for cattle but only one for tule elk.

Out With the BIRDS

The Cardinal
Photo by A. Pursley

By Ernest S. Booth

Few people today realize that 75 years ago bird study was the number one hobby in America. If one goes to a large library and examines bird books, he discovers that scores of bird books were published back in the 1890's, written by men who spent most of their time with the birds.

Bird egg collecting seemed to trigger this unusual interest, but the oologists, as they were called, did much more than collect eggs. They were the forerunners of modern bird watchers. They pioneered bird photography and made some of the finest photographs of the day, working with meager equipment and poor film. Many authors produced veritable encyclopedias of bird lore, perhaps three or four deluxe volumes, such as *Birds of California* by William Leon Dawson. This was the golden age of ornithology.

But bird study has changed a good deal. Federal laws protecting birds, nests and eggs (1918) made it almost impossible for people to pursue egg collecting as a hobby, so bird students turned more to observation of the birds themselves for their pleasure. Bird watching as a leisure time activity provided the dual pleasure of a rewarding hobby and the joy of visiting the woods and fields in the early morning. Many found great satisfaction in walking along a deserted beach in a rainstorm to observe migrating shorebirds. The hobby, in a more sophisticated form, really became popular during the 1940's and 1950's, and it is estimated that today there are nearly five million bird watchers in America.

A bird student cannot be successful unless he works by himself much of the time. You must be alone in order to know birds. With even one other person, you will see less than half as many birds than if you are alone.

Bird watching has other rewards too. Sunshine is pleasant, but a snowstorm in a forest is actually exciting. A trek on skis through a forest in winter with the snow ten feet deep is an experience not soon forgotten. Only a few birds are usually seen during that season, but they are as important to know as any.

The fresh smell of the woods, of rocky shores or of the jungle is another of nature's pleasant allurements. Nature sounds take a lifetime to learn. I often carry a tape recorder to bring the sounds of nature back to study. Another joy has been learning the songs of birds. By patient and careful listening, I learned to recognize every bird in Washington State by sound alone. By repeated sound and sight observation, I have come to know many of the birds of Mexico by sound. It

White-breasted Nuthatch
Photo by Donald Pfitzer

Hawaiian Booby
Photo by Ernest S. Booth

Wild Mallard
Photo by Lloyd Beesley

is always exciting to hear a new sound and then spend the next hour tracking down the creature making the sound. This is an important part of the game which never ends, for elusive songs need to be heard again and again before they become part of your bird lore.

Birds take one away from civilization to the remote corners of the earth—to the tops of high mountains, along rugged shores, into torrid jungles, to the arctic tundra or into the burning desert. I gladly follow them to these places. To see my life list pass 1700 was thrilling, and to have my U.S.A. list reach 622 was equally exciting. But listing birds is not the only important thing; rather, it is the sum total of the experiences one has while finding those 1700 species that really counts. It is the lure of travel, seeing unknown places, becoming one with the wilderness that are the true rewards of bird watching.

If this description has succeeded in capturing your imagination, perhaps you would like to become a bird watcher. You could begin this hobby in any number of ways, one of which is suggested here.

First, purchase a good pair of binoculars. A good pair will be more rewarding in the long run. They need not be expensive, but check them out carefully. Make a few tests. A good test is to focus on a distant tree to see if the binoculars will pick out individual leaves clearly. If the leaves are sharp and clear, the binoculars will serve you suitably. Also see that they are in focus to the edges of the field.

If you have a strong neck, you might prefer a 7×50, the large size which lets in more light than smaller binoculars. But if you don't like that weight around your neck for hours on end, then pick a 7×35. A six-power glass might be better for elderly people than a seven-power, for the higher power needs steadier hands so that the bird does not seem to dance around.

Get the largest objective lens possible, for

that determines how much light will reach
you from the bird. This is why 7×50
is the best of all. The 7, of course, denotes
magnification; the 50 indicates a 50 millimeter
lens diameter. A 35 millimeter diameter
is next best, but less than this is rather poor.
Central focusing is especially important; do
not buy a glass with only individual eye
focusing. Wide angle glasses are not comfortable
because they strain your eyes to take in
too much territory.

Select one or more of the several good
bird guides on the market. You need not carry
them into the woods. Instead, carry a small
notebook to jot down descriptions and other
details about the birds seen. Look up each
bird in your guide later. It's best to keep a
loose-leaf notebook with a page for each kind of
bird. Record all observations about that kind
of bird and add more pages as you need
them. You will be amazed how your knowledge
of birds grows if you keep a good notebook.

A spotting scope is excellent for studying
waterfowl, hawks or any bird that is
perched or is stationary a distance away. Since
a tripod must be used, a scope is of little
value with birds flitting around in treetops.

The main prerequisite for a new bird watcher
is a strong curosity about birds and a
willingness to look for birds at any time and
under all conditions. He will want to keep
a yearly list and a life list. If these lists are
not kept, enthusiasm for the hobby will
diminish. Other lists are also interesting, such
as a list of birds seen on one particular trip,
or the most birds seen in one day.

Try some of the special study methods,
too, such as bird photography and sound
recording. Both of these are more expensive, so
your finances will determine how far you go
with photography and recording. Today,
however, with the low cost portable recorders
you may do sound recording for less than
$100 investment. Bird photography requires
a good quality camera which can take a strong

Recording bird sounds on location.

Binoculars are basic to field observation.

Out with the BIRDS

telephoto lens. Cost for such equipment amounts to $500 and more. Used equipment of top quality from a reputable store is a better investment than new equipment of medium or low quality.

Some may be interested in birdbanding. This requires a knowledge about birds and proficiency at identification. A federal banding permit is required.

But how may one begin the fascinating hobby of bird watching without binoculars, cameras and the like? You can start in your own backyard, with a feeding table and birdbath outside your kitchen window. Place shrubs and trees in your yard so that birds can dodge cats and dogs and feel at home around your house. Get acquainted with the best bird study haunts in your area—rivers, streams, wooded areas, forests, shores, lakes and meadows. Travel as much as possible, to national parks and monuments and other interesting areas. Wildlife refuges are always outstanding spots for bird study. Then there are often special areas made famous because of some unusual condition. Such places as Hawk Mountain, Cape May, the Everglades, Malheur Lake, Klamath Lakes, Great Salt Lake, Arkansas Refuge and many others are famous.

The important points to remember are: (1) Determine the degree of interest you have in bird watching. (2) Follow a system for recording your lists and other observations. (3) Equip yourself with whatever is needed to pursue the hobby in the manner you prefer and can afford. (4) Enjoy bird watching as you learn.

Photo by Donald Pfitzer

The Red-tailed HAWK

By D. Rexford Lord
Photography by Dan Sudia

The magnificence of the red-tailed hawk is due primarily to its handsome attire and its agility in flight. Although a heavy bird with a wingspan of nearly five feet, it has a flawless grace as its swoops to earth to gather its prey. Its massive appearance cannot be better illustrated on film or canvass than in the Dan Sudia portrait on the opposite page.

The red-tailed hawk is known by two scientific names. The correct name is *Buteo jamaicensis* which indicates that the earliest known specimen was probably collected on or near the island of Jamaica. The older name *Buteo borealis,* while no longer acceptable to ornithologists, is somehow more appropriate since this name refers to its distribution over the North American continent.

The bird has been given several common names. Red-tailed hawk is clearly the best name since it is descriptive and rules out confusion with other species. It sometimes is called hen hawk and white-breasted chicken hawk. The name "chicken hawk" has been applied to the red-tailed hawk probably more than to any other species simply because it is so abundant and of a size capable of capturing a chicken. However, scientific studies clearly reveal that it is unjustly accused.

Hawks and certainly redtails have always been renowned for their excellent eyesight. The eye of a bird is far more than just a precision optical instrument. Unlike man-made optics, the eyes of birds and mammals must be dynamically adaptable. Lighting conditions and distances to focus upon are constantly changing as the animal moves. This requires constant changes in the aperture of the pupil and the focus through the lens onto the retina. Tiny muscles achieve these needs. The opening of the pupil is changed by circularly and radially aligned muscles located in the iris, the part of the eye which imparts color to it. Focus is achieved by changing the curvature of the lens. In mammals these actions are achieved by smooth muscle, a primitive type of muscle notoriously slow in reacting, but in birds these muscles are striated, quick acting and powerful.

Red-tailed hawks and other hawks have achieved the ultimate in visual adaptation. Man, we know, has binocular vision; both eyes focus on the objective together. This arrangement permits the best perception of depth available in an optical system limited to two points of observation. Birds (except owls) have their eyes located on the sides of their heads. This way all degrees of the compass are in view. Hawks, however, have a special requirement. They must be able to accurately judge the distance to the prey on the ground. One mistake in the wrong direction could result in the bird's crashing into the ground or missing the prey. Thus binocular vision is invaluable to hawks.

The eyes of hawks contain two special areas of central focus called the foveae. Man has one fovea and so do most birds. But hawks have two, one for uniocular vision and the other for binocular vision. For the "stoop" (the dive of a hawk or falcon upon its prey), binocular vision becomes imperative. And for great distance eyesight the central fovea, uniocular vision, is the best. To shift uniocular vision to binocular vision, hawks have a special muscle which "cocks" the lens—slightly refocusing the fovea for binocular vision.

Red-tailed hawks lay two to five eggs per clutch, and usually raise only one family each year. There is a high rate of infant mortality. However, once a hawk attains maturity, it probably will survive considerably longer. The average longevity is 1-2/3 years.

The nests, high in tall trees, are constructed of large sticks at the base and finer materials to line the nest, often ending with fresh greenery. Generations of nests may be superimposed annually.

A few redtails pass the winter in the northern tier of states, but most of them winter in the south to the tropics. There is an obvious concentration of red-tailed hawks in winter on the coastal plains of Texas, especially on the rice fields west of Houston. Here they subsist principally on grasshoppers. Elsewhere, rodents form the principal basis of their diet. They eat whatever is easily obtained. Their food varies from field mice to ground squirrels with occasional feasts on pheasants, quail, chickens and rabbits.

The red-tailed hawk is a massive, graceful and handsomely attired bird—one well worth close observance by any bird watcher.

Twenty-nine years ago, back in the hidden marshlands of White Lake, Louisiana, a flock of eight whooping cranes fought for survival. Only 22 whooping cranes, including this flock, remained on earth.

With their black-tipped wings outstretched, they skimmed over the sand trumpeting a wild and primitive cry. Dropping lightly to earth, they stood 5 feet tall on long, delicate legs. With carmine-crowned heads held high, eyes alert, they scanned their domain.

A young female tugged reeds from the mud as though practicing nest building. While she worked, the sky darkened. Muddy waters churned at her feet. Wind ripped her feathers. She and the other cranes stalked about nervously.

The wind blew into a hurricane. It flattened the reeds and tall grass. Waves slowly flooded the marshlands.

One by one the birds, including the young female, spread their enormous wings and were swept into the gray sky. She was the only female of the flock to survive the storm.

With a broken wing, she dropped exhausted into a rice field. Warily, she watched a farmer coming toward her. He approached her slowly and spoke softly. Later, he brought food and water to her.

The lost crane forgot her fears and responded to the farmer's care. The farmer soon determined that the bird was very unusual though he, at first, thought her to be a common crane. For her own safety, she was taken to the New Orleans Zoo as soon as she was well enough.

There she was placed in a narrow cage. The card in front read, "Josephine . . . whooping crane . . . very rare and priceless."

For 8 years, Josephine peered through the wires looking for a mate, but she saw only curious visitors staring back.

Later she was taken from her cage and brought to the Aransas Game Refuge in Texas to meet Pete.

Pete had been shot in an eye and a wing many years prior to their meeting. Though rescued, he seemed not to forget the injuries and was aloof and unfriendly in his Nebraska Zoo home.

Now, in the enclosed wilderness area of 150 acres, the two captives were released.

Josephine delighted in her freedom and ran through tall yellow grass snatching grasshoppers and other insects. She darted to the water's edge to snare a little sideways-crawling blue crab; and there she saw . . . Old Pete. He was strutting stiff-legged along the shore.

With his one injured wing and one gleaming amber eye, he looked fierce and masculine.

THE WHOOPING CRANES

By Jean Bartenbach
Photography by Donald F. Pfitzer, unless otherwise indicated

Color pictures accompanying this article
are actual photos of Josephine.

But Josephine leaped for joy. She twirled,
dipped and skipped.

Pete seemed to forget both his age and his
dignity and bounded about on the ground around
her. They danced in the yellow grass, they
danced on the salt flats, and they danced in the
mud.

Within a few days they began weaving a
nest of salt grass, carefully hiding it in the
dense, narrow-leaved cattails. In the nest, Josephine laid two eggs. Pete stood guard. He
chased away some Louisiana herons, egrets,
spoonbills and even fought a rattlesnake. Pete
was rather old for all this constant chasing about
in the mud.

After 3 weeks he nudged Josephine off the
nest. Together they poked and turned the eggs.
The eggs were infertile. They pecked them open
and destroyed them.

Josephine planned to start another family at
once. She coaxed Pete to the open meadow where
they again danced.

But Pete was too old and tired. He sank into
the shallow water of the salt pond and didn't
get up.

Josephine stood alone on the salt flats and
called and called, but Pete was dead.

For a long while Josephine grieved for Pete
and for her unborn chicks.

Josephine

Three months passed, and the remembrance of Pete grew dim.

One morning Josephine was feeding at the edge of the lagoon when there appeared in the water's reflection a handsome whooping crane.

Josephine raised her graceful head and saw —Crip.

Crip had been found with a broken wing on the wintering marshlands and had been brought to share the refuge with Josephine.

Josephine was delighted.

The two splendid birds became immediate friends. Together they built a nest on the open flats. In it Josephine laid a single egg. Happily she sat on the nest, and Crip fought off all intruders.

In 4 weeks the egg cracked open. A little rust-colored chick struggled out of the egg and wobbled from the nest. Josephine hovered over her chick. Crip tenderly poked bits of food into its tiny beak.

Little Rusty romped about, tottering and tumbling over the feet of his joyful parents.

On the third day their joy ended abruptly.

In a cold gray rain, the little chick wandered a short distance away and disappeared. Josephine and Crip called through the cattails and searched in the grass. They poked at the soggy nest with the bits of eggshell still clinging to it, and they searched in the mud. There they saw raccoon tracks mixed with tiny scurrying toeprints, and they knew the tragic end of Rusty.

Josephine whooped mournfully. Crip stayed close to her.

The following spring, on a small bit of marshy ground surrounded by water, they built another nest. And Josephine laid another egg.

A storm gathered. Blinding rain swept across the marsh. The tide rose. Water slowly crept to the edge of the nest.

Frantically Josephine and Crip labored to build up the sides, but it was a losing battle. The egg floated from the nest and shattered against the reeds.

Josephine and Crip were taken back to the New Orleans Zoo where Josephine's future eggs would be protected from mishap.

Photo by Luther C. Goldman
Courtesy of U.S. Department of the Interior.

Josephine

But Josephine, seeming not to care any more, stopped laying eggs—eggs necessary to carry on her kind. She dragged around the enclosure behind the elephant cage nibbling at her food and ignoring Crip.

In 1951, after 14 years of strict protection, the whooping crane population stood at only 25. The margin of survival remained perilously thin.

Five years passed.

Suddenly, one day, the force of instinct seemed to surge through Josephine. She flapped her wings, arched her neck and bounced over to Crip.

Crip was elated. He rose up on his toes, spread his huge wings and sprang into the air. Together they danced.

Josephine began pulling bits of straw into a corner of the cage. She built a nest, and in it she laid an egg.

Reporters and photographers came to witness the big event. Visitors bustled up to the cage. Someone thoughtlessly poked a stick through the wires. Josephine became frightened and left the nest. Crip, backing up to protect it, accidentally stepped on the egg and smashed it.

Josephine's ill-fated attempts at raising a family apparently failed to discourage her.

The following spring, without bothering to build a nest, Josephine laid an egg on the bare ground. Four days later she laid another egg beside the first.

While she sat, she pulled bits of straw around them. Within a month a small wet chick emerged from the first egg.

Josephine and Crip put their beaks together and trumpeted their success to the world.

In a few days, the second egg hatched. During the night a large owl glided silently into the cage and swooped off with the tiny new chick.

The parents, dismayed to find it gone, turned all their attention to the firstborn. They stayed close beside the chick and fed him insects flushed from the grass.

The chick grew rapidly.

During the July heat, the little crane seemed to tire easily. One afternoon he sat panting beneath the camphor tree and suddenly toppled over. He died from an infection of the lungs.

He had lived 6 weeks.

Concern over the loss of the chicks was felt around the world. Everyone mourned with the parents who were struggling so hard to save their species.

For Josephine, time was getting short. The chance of having her own family was becoming more remote. That spring, ahead of schedule, she started her annual effort to raise young.

On a small pad of hay she laid two eggs.

One month later two chicks broke out of the shells. In an hour they were dry and fluffy and had tottered 6 feet from the nest.

Josephine quickly gathered them under her wings. Now and then a small fuzzy head popped out of its feather bed and looked around. Crip rushed over to drop food into the open beak. Then Josephine would prod the little crane back under her wing.

For 5 days and nights Crip stayed awake and alert to danger, and Josephine kept the chicks close to her.

This time no harm came.

The brown-eyed, cinnamon-colored chicks were healthy from the start. They ate constantly. In 1 week they were 7 inches tall.

They played together and frisked about on long skinny legs and feet.

Hopefully, the chicks were named George and Georgette. This was later changed to George I and George II. They were the first whooping cranes ever to be hatched, and survive in captivity.

The following spring Josephine hatched and raised another baby crane named Pee-Wee.

Encouraged by her success, Josephine began laying eggs with abandon. Most were infertile. Three hatched but none of the babies survived.

Josephine

Three years and many eggs later, Pepper, the last of Josephine's chicks was hatched and lived. In all, four of her chicks have grown to maturity.

In 1964 Josephine died of natural causes. She had lived 25 years. She had a lifespan three times longer than normal for wild cranes. Her chicks, along with several new captives, have been successful parents only a few times.

None has been as productive as Josephine who earned her title as "Queen of the Whooping Cranes."

It is hoped that present research coupled with the fierce will and family pride of the cranes will aid them in successfully rearing their young in captivity. Each bird is a vital link in the survival of the species.

After several years of effort and research, an extraordinary plan has been undertaken to assist in the reproduction of wild whooping cranes.

A helicopter swoops down into the remote regions of northwest Canada, the summer nesting site of the birds. With great care, one egg is taken from each nest where there are two in a nest. It has already been determined that only one of the two eggs ever has a chance to survive in the wilds.

These eggs are flown at once to the Patuxent Wildlife Research Center in Maryland. The eggs are taken to the incubator where they are kept safe and snug, away from predators and bad weather.

In June 1967, five healthy baby chicks popped out of the shells. The airlift operation was a triumphant success. The incubator-hatched whoopers presently number 10.

The total number of whooping cranes both wild and in captivity now stands at an encouraging 50. A species on the edge of extinction is slowly and hopefully enduring.

Photo by W. F. Kubichek. Courtesy of U.S. Department of the Interior

a SPOONBILL is a SPOONBILL

By Mike Smith
Photography by the Author

These beautiful pink birds appear to be making a comeback from near extinction.

Fifty thousand tourists can be wrong!

Flamingos they are not—the peppermint-pink birds with the green tablespoon bills that feed in the ponds of Everglades National Park at the foot of Florida.

The pink birds are roseate spoonbills, *Ajaia ajaja,* to be scientific, and are kin to the ibis. They measure 28 to 31 inches from bill tip to tail feathers and have a wingspread of 48 to 53 inches.

Only 25 years ago the roseate spoonbill was a vanishing species, highly endangered, first, by predatory plume hunters, and then by the winds of progress that blow even in the vastness of the Everglades and across the isolated mangrove islands where spoonbills like to breed.

Early this year visitors to Everglades National Park saw evidence of a remarkable comeback of this pink bird.

As the morning sunlight burned the gray mists from Myrazk Pond, a shallow brackish lake bordering the east shoulder of Highway 27 two miles from Flamingo, Florida, flocks of roseate spoonbills came gliding from the light-filled sky to feed in the insect-dimpled water.

On almost any winter morning, and on many afternoons, too, bemused bird watchers stand on the bank beside the road and see from a score to half a hundred of the heron-sized birds wading in the shallow yellow-brown water only a few feet from the highway. The birds feed on aquatic insects, shrimp or small fish by swishing their bills back and forth as they walk in widening half circles of ripples. Sometimes they dip their heads completely underwater. Now and then they lift them and eye the visitors with unconcern. Occasionally they leave the water to perch on stumps and dry their wings or to walk along the

The spoonbill, although sometimes confused with the flamingo, can be easily recognized by its bill, which is shaped like a flattened tablespoon and is about six inches long. The spoonbill is also much paler in color, with the darker pink plumage on the wings.

By comparing a flamingo with a spoonbill, it is obvious that the only resemblance is the color of the plumage.

53

SPOONBILL

racks of hurricane-killed trees that border three sides of the pond.

"Look at the flamingos," visitors whisper in awe, unlimbering binoculars and long lenses for their cameras.

"Roseate spoonbills," Floridians correct. But the correction is useless. A tourist knows a flamingo when he sees one. A flamingo is a large pink bird. These are large pink birds. Therefore, tourists assume they are flamingos.

The only resemblance between a flamingo and a spoonbill is the color of the plumage. A spoonbill is a spoonbill, and it does not look very much like any other of the 326 species of birds observed in the 2,100-square-mile park, the third largest in the United States. Indeed the spoonbill appears to be constructed of spare parts, odds and ends left over from other birds and some beasts. The wings of the adult are as pink as sunset clouds, and the plumage has a satin sheen. The stubby tail is a gorgeous orange, and the bird wears epaulets of crimson. Its bill, about six inches long and shaped like a flattened tablespoon, is a palmetto green mottled with gray. The spoonbill's head is bald except for ear patches of black. Its gleaming red eyes hold an extraordinary look of friendliness.

Although the roseate spoonbill has a claim to remarkable beauty in its plumage, the effect of the bird's appearance is not one of total elegance. It appears somewhat like a friendly little old man with a green Jimmy Durante nose, who unaccountably found himself clad in a pink tutu, hearing aids and old sneakers.

At present there are about 500 adult spoonbills in the Everglades National Park. They are year-round residents and nest on remote mangrove islands in the Florida Bay region. Probably there are a thousand more elsewhere in Florida. The pink bird's range is from southern Texas, Louisiana, Alabama and Georgia to Argentina.

In 1858 the birds were abundant on Pelican Island in the Indian River, and in 1874 they were seen breeding along the shore of Lake Okeechobee. As late as 1931 a game warden saw 1,000 along the southwest coast of Florida. Today the birds are on the U.S. Fish and Wildlife Service's rare and endangered species list, along with the great white heron, bald eagle, whooping crane and other birds.

But the gathering of the roseate spoonbills and other birds at Myrazk Pond during the first three months of this year proved the birds are increasing in number. It also branded as a half-truth the old aphorism, "Birds of a feather flock together." It was apparent even to the casual observer that birds not of a feather also flock together. Feeding happily with the spoonbills were at least a hundred wood storks, dozens of snow-white American egrets, a score of golden-slippered snowy egrets, a few blue herons and Louisiana herons, a fussy green heron, a great blue heron and a rare white heron. In the middle of the pond floated a line composed of about six white pelicans, huge birds that are visitors from the Pacific coast. Black skimmers fled over the surface of the shallow water, scooping fish into their bills. Ducks and coots swam with the pelicans. Anhingas dried their wings on stumps and trees. Immature ibis waded near the shore.

It was a spectacular bird show, but its star was the roseate spoonbill—not the flamingo.

THE CROW DOTH SING

But he usually reserves his "singing" till he's alone in the deep woods

By Thomas F. Monser
Photo by the Author

One of the more intelligent birds is the common crow. It wouldn't have surprised me if the first astronaut to set foot on the moon had reported that he saw crows up there. Crow history is recorded way back to ancient times. In an old illustrated manuscript written in Syria about 1200, the King of Crows is shown listen- ing to advice from his counselors on how to deal with owls.

His wisdom is the result of a long and exceptionally sly relationship with man. Watch one inspecting a row of corn that has just sprouted. He proudly steps off a pace that transmits the impression he's the one who planted the corn in the first place, in soil that is rightfully his.

Count the scarecrows on a hunk of acreage that's been planted with seed corn, and you'll find several crows using these hideous-looking figures for a perch. Confidentially, if a farmer would only tar his seeds, he would force them to feed elsewhere.

Shakespeare stated a natural history fact when he had Portia utter to Nerissa, "The crow doth sing as sweetly as the lark when neither is attended." The crow does save his song for a time when he's well hidden in the deep woods.

I found this out one summer day. I concealed myself behind a huge oak tree to watch a pair of gray squirrels playing tag. The two rodents circled the tree trunk with the female constantly in the lead. Round and round they went, hugging the bark and flashing their large banner tails. The male would almost catch up with the object of his affection, but she wasn't to be caught napping.

I heard a warbling sound blending in with the breeze. At intervals it was like the low, gurgling calls a starling indulges in. I stood up, changing my position, covering the action with my field glasses, trying to find the noisemaker.

Just below me a spruce tree with many branches stuck out among the hardwoods. I saw five crows hunched up, perched in a row, and sitting like old men relating exaggerated stories of their youth. A crow would warble, then others in turn repeated the refrain.

I mentioned the incident to Arthur A. Allen, the world's first professor of ornithology, during an interview at his laboratory in Ithaca, New York, a short time before his death.

"You've been treated to a rare incident," he told me. "Few people have been fortunate enough to hear a crow sing. You are lucky."

The crow is not a solitary bird. He likes company. More than likely, wherever you see him feeding, you'll see another crow acting as sentinel. His diet is varied and he isn't beyond picking through the stuff spread by a farmer's "honey wagon" to fertilize his field. Possibly this is what Forbush meant when he said, "The crow knows a good thing when he sees it. He seeks the bounty of the field."

The versatile crow performs a beneficial service to human beings with the amount of carrion he consumes. Dead rabbits, woodchucks and raccoons are favorite dishes. He will also eat reptiles, wild fruit in season, nuts, grasshoppers, beetles, grubs, frogs, salamanders and once in a while a fledgling or two. He will push the owlets of the great horned owl out of their nest if left unguarded.

He is an early riser. Long before you think about crawling out of your warm bed, he and his pals have gathered together at a dumping site and are busy eating leftovers. He isn't particular how old the stuff is either. I have counted over one hundred birds at these feasting places, clamoring and wedging their way through the crowd searching for food.

In the forest he keeps a sharp eye for any creature that moves. He and his pals will follow a red fox on his rounds, in order to be able to glean a few scraps from his kill.

One bitter cold afternoon I surprised a pair of foxes feeding on a rabbit. The animals weren't alarmed at all when I came over a hill and looked down at them. They stared at me and then continued to feed. I was at least 30 yards away. I wondered how close I could get before they would become disturbed. Walking slowly in their direction but careful not to startle them, I went fifteen more steps before they loped away, looking at me over their shoulders. When I examined the carcass of the rabbit, there was still some flesh left on the bones.

I heard a crow calling. Another answered. Both were sitting in an elm tree near the edge of the woods. The two imps had been waiting for the foxes to leave. I crossed just below them and walked silently into the woods, circling back to my starting point to check on the hungry pair. When I got back where I could see, one crow was on the ground feeding on the discarded rabbit while the other remained on watch.

Another time I watched a buck deer walking along a trail that led through a hemlock grove. The animal stopped near a small sapling to scrape the velvet from his horns. Three crows followed him. They perched in a tree just above the deer, cawing and carrying on until quite a few crows had gathered. The buck was apparently looking for a day bed, but became so upset with the uproar that he bolted and ran through the woods with the crows flying after him.

The crow isn't a tiny bird. He reaches a length of twenty inches and has a wingspread up to thirty. His size leaves him with few natural enemies, the most formidable being the great horned owl. This feathered glutton will raid a crow roost, winging his hushed way through the air with less noise than dust falling on your maple leaf table. Until the crows are able to drive him from their territory, the owl manages to freeze the plasma in their blood as they shiver and shake on a branch listening to his paralyzing hunting call. He delivers a verbal barrage of banshee calls, hoping to frighten a crow into betraying his hideout by some sound or movement.

The crow is thus frightened and helpless at night; but when the light of day returns, his aggressive attitude also comes back. It's his turn to rattle the composure out of the owl and teach him a thing or two about peaceful coexistence.

He does this with the help of his eager band. Discovering his enemy sitting hidden in a tree, the crow, with his flashing wings, dives directly in front of the owl and delivers a quick jab on the top of his head. Each bird in the flock in turn hovers over the owl's back, jamming down with his sharp beak. The owl doesn't like this treatment and flies away. The crows usually give chase. I have seen this happen many times.

One day I heard a flock worrying an owl in this way. Then there was silence as they flew away. I saw the owl sitting on a large branch next to the trunk of a beech tree. Only half of his body was visible. In my effort to move closer I alarmed him, and he flew. A black shadow from the top of another tree followed him. It was a lone crow who had been left behind by the flock for the specific task of keeping track of the owl. This is used to keep the flock tuned in for a day of fun whenever they decide to resume their game. They don't actually do the owl much harm, but if one ever connects with the owl's talons or curved beak, the crow usually leaves this world quite suddenly, with no provision made for his progeny.

In the early spring when the flocks return from the South, they pair off. The males show their strength by flying erratically through the air while an interested female watches from a perch. Should a rival male wing into the area, he is quickly chased away by the first suitor. They peck at each other for a short time. Most of their belligerency is confined to pursuit.

Crows make a crude nest. Twigs and branches are simply stacked together into a bowl-like shape. How a female crow can be comfortable sitting on such a pile of wood is a mystery.

Complete silence is kept when the crows are nesting. They arrive down a flyway to their nest in a very quiet manner, taking every precaution not to be seen.

When the young hatch, they are fed constantly. Three weeks later they leave the nest to tag along with their parents, begging for food even after they are quite capable of finding their own. If you have ever heard the ranting cry of one of these little bounders pestering the old crows for something to eat, you'd know why they give in without too much hesitation. The noise irritates your eardrums.

Immature crows join the rest of the crow community in the early fall and begin learning the rules the flock lives by. They are taught wing drill, the various calls used in crow language and sentry duty. And they soon learn the difference between a gun or a stick.

I watched a flock doing wing drills one fall day. About 30 birds participated. They were scattered in all directions but soon bunched together again, dropping as one unit to the ground. Then back up in the tree they went. Three crows flew out again. Straight up into the air they went, leveling off and diving straight down, landing back in the tree. As if on signal, the entire flock copied the maneuver.

Corvus brachyrhynchos, the common crow, does migrate after a fashion. He leaves the northernmost part of his range for warmer areas where food is more abundant. Birders hate to see him leave each fall and welcome his return in the spring. May he continue to increase. Our world would be a less pleasant place to be if we didn't have the crow to jazz up the stillness over a brooding landscape with his more than welcome "caw, caw, caw."

THE CROW DOTH SING

The
PERFORMER

That Daring Mimic,
the Blue Jay

by Thomas F. Monser

Dan Sudia

As I was walking deep in the heart of a pine forest one day, I noticed a red squirrel as he jumped from a branch to the top of a stone wall. He ran, then stopped and stared at me. I didn't move, and he was soon satisfied that all was well and continued about his business, chattering and squealing away. An answering voice came from the branches of a pine tree just ahead of me. I was expecting another squirrel to show up, but instead a blue jay hopped out on a limb, raised and lowered his crest, cocked his head and duplicated the red squirrel's chatter. The blue-jacketed mimic gave a perfect performance. I remembered how many times in the past he had fooled me with other calls.

Once I was watching a flicker chip out a new home in a dead hickory tree. The site was in the shadow of a huge beech where a pair of red-tailed hawks had taken over an abandoned crow's nest. The male hawk sat in a tree a short distance away, his glassy eyes riveted in a blank expression.

Suddenly the wild, piercing, high-pitched cry of a red-tailed hawk split the silence. I looked up at the male and saw the same blank expression. I thought I had missed his giving the sound, so I watched him, hoping to catch him in the act. The sound came once more, but he did not make it, and his mate sat quietly in the nearby nest. A shadow moving in the trees attracted my attention. I was expecting another hawk, but a blue jay appeared through the leaves and before I could gather my thoughts he delivered a perfect call of a red-tailed hawk.

Armchair naturalists condemn the blue jay as a habitual plunderer of bird's eggs and young, but actually most of his food consists of vegetable matter, such as acorns, beech nuts and hickory nuts. For appetizers he prefers wood-boring beetles, grasshoppers and eggs of various caterpillars, which most birds will not touch. The remainder of his diversified menu includes scale insects, mice, fish, salamanders, snails and some crustaceans.

A jay can hack a nut to shreds, ripping out the meat. However, much of the time he is eating last year's crop which has been softened after being covered by wet leaves. Holding the nut between both feet, he pounds away at the shell, jabbing at it with his daggerlike bill.

I once saw a jay work on an especially tough acorn. He hit the shell so many times without cracking it that his bill must have been getting sore. He finally picked up the nut in his beak and flew to a nearby log where he wedged the acorn in a crack and hammered the shell off. All this trouble for an acorn!

The blue jay is quite jealous of anyone taking food from what he considers his private cupboard. For instance, one chilly autumn day while I was gathering beech nuts after several frosts had opened the burrs, a blue jay appeared and, seeing me, shrieked "jay, jay, jay" in rapid succession, bobbing up and down. His call sounded more like "thief, thief, thief," and I felt like one. The entire time I was there collecting the nuts, other jays continued to harass me.

Blue jays are also greedy as evidenced by an encounter I witnessed after flushing a flock of slate-colored juncos from underneath a wild grape vine. A chickadee was busy feeding on the grapes. He yanked a grape loose, then flew to a nearby spot to eat it. He was soon joined by several other members of his species. They tossed about a rapid series of "dee-dee-dee" calls. Without warning, a louder chickadee call rang out, and a blue jay came upon the scene, imitating the fluid song of the chickadee.

He suddenly flashed out of a hawthorn bush, flying directly at the chickadees. I thought, this is it, the blue bomber is going to nab one of those black-capped birds. Just before reaching them, the jay turned and flew back to his perch. He repeated this caper until the chickadees became so upset they flew

away, leaving the blue jay to feast happily on the wild grapes without having to share them.

The blue jay's prime trait is his curiosity, which compels him to investigate everything that occurs in the forest. He seems to enjoy spying on other birds and animals and he moves silently about, prying into their affairs. Even though they do not like him around, they heed his warning whistle.

On one extremely cold morning in the middle of winter, I was following the fresh imprints of a white-tailed deer, hoping to catch the elusive animal lying in his day bed. I moved slowly against the wind so the deer would not catch my scent. I paced my steps in a stop, look and walk pattern, and I knew if I did not push too hard, the deer would bed down.

The flash of a blue jay's wings moved across my field of vision. The bird's sudden appearance startled me, and I stopped, tingling with boiling desperation. If the jay became alarmed, my plan would be ruined, for every deer within range of his voice would be long gone into another county.

The bird moved closer, his top knot moving up and down with each movement. If he flattened it, I knew that he was about to broadcast my presence. He flew from branch to branch and hopped up and down looking for moth eggs. I was sure now that he was not alarmed. Then he stopped feeding and looked back at me, cocking his head. His blue feathers glistened, and the spots on his wings and tail were as white as the snow. He whistled softly, "kloo-loo-loo." I relaxed, positive that I had put one over on the blue jay, but he fooled me. He flew to the top of a tree and gave his cry of danger. A loud, crashing sound in the thick growth just ahead told me the deer had heeded the bird's warning cry.

Some blue jays migrate to a warmer climate during the winter, but hardier individuals remain in the Northern states and spend much of their time looking for food. It is no problem attracting them to your bird feeder, for they relish sunflower seeds.

Henry David Thoreau wrote in 1850: "I hear deep amid the birches some row among the birds or the squirrels, where evidently some mystery is being developed to them. The jay is on the alert, mimicking every woodland note." The woods would not be the same without the blue jay. May he continue to shatter the silence of the forest with his varied calls.

ERWINGS

Drummer of the Forest

Story and Photography by Harvey Hansen
Painting by Jim Padgett

Frequently in the springtime woods a "you-come-find-me" sound beats intriguingly upon my ears. Part of it resembles distant thunder; most of it reminds me of a small engine that won't quite start. Far or near, it seems to have about the same volume. Only when I am close does the sound become noticeably louder. And just when I think I am close enough to see what is making such a mysterious noise, the sound stops altogether.

This brief, frequently repeated sound is heard by many outdoor people. But not many know positively that it is the drumming of a male ruffed grouse; fewer know how he does it.

Common opinion credits the grouse with abilities that would outperform a double-jointed, one-man band. Opinion says he drums by beating his wings against a hollow log or hollow stump, or by beating his wings on his chest, and even by beating them behind his back. My first, rather distant, observation also gave me the impression that his wings beat behind his back. It looked that way to my unaided eyes, whether the grouse was viewed from front or back. It looked nearly the opposite to Audubon! He said the grouse "beats its sides with its wings in the manner of a domestic cock."

Differing opinions indicate that grouse deserve study. Each spring during the past 6 years I have spent hundreds of hours observing them in northern Wisconsin where I live. Here the drumming season usually lasts from mid-April to mid-June. By June the action occurs less often and starts later in the day. Especially from late April to late May, a grouse drums several sessions a day beginning as early as 3 o'clock in the morning and ending shortly before sundown. Some grouse perform 2 or 3 hours into the night, and some probably have sessions all through any mild, moon-bright night.

A single session lasts from a few minutes to a couple of hours with Mr. Thunderwings performing every 2 to 5 minutes. During the minutes before performances, he usually stands on the drumming spot looking about alertly. If the weather is warm, he pants from his exertions and may distend his feathers to let in any cool breezes. In cold weather, he stands looking plump. Sometimes he lets his wings hang down, then quickly snaps them to his sides like a soldier coming to attention.

If any unusual or unexpected sound occurs or a small bird flits close by, he instantly shrinks, by contracting his feathers, to seemingly half his size. After a while, if he is not scared away and no further disturbance occurs, he resumes drumming—but it is whisper soft. When an "all-is-well" feeling returns, his drumming becomes so powerful that it actually can be felt some distance away. I have felt the beats reverberating in my chest.

Occasionally he scoots off the log to administer demise to a tasty insect and then immediately returns to drumming. Or, like an epicure sampling foods from many tables, he spends several minutes filling his crop with leaves from almost every plant or bush he walks by, including some stems of young bracken fern gobbled from tip to ground in a series of quick snips. When he is full, he may sit still for several minutes.

Moments of scratching and preening himself and turning around on the drumming spot signal that Mr. Thunderwings will soon leave—to eat, to rest or to try his luck at another location. He usually has two to four favorite spots. One grouse I watched had eight sites, including the cement corner of an abandoned foundation. This was entirely grown over with moss, bracken and small balsam, except for the one bare corner. Mr. Thunderwings often drummed there with his toes hooked over the front edge of the cement.

Other spots I have seen drummers use include a hump of sod, an up-jutting root, the top trunk of three bare and crisscrossed aspen windfalls and moss-covered logs. Often when leaving a drumming site, the drummer walks direct and fast, like a man meeting an appointment on time, or he runs as if winning a hundred-yard dash.

Ruffed grouse (Bonasa umbellus) occupy some of the southern states and much of the northern half of the United States, the southern half of Canada and eastern Alaska.

The whole thunderous show of a male grouse drumming is something to behold! With the help of a blind, some cameras and a tape recorder, I determined wing positions and sound details previously unnoticed by my unaided eyes and ears.

First, he hops onto a favorite log and walks to his chosen drumming spot. There he stands, chickenlike, and looks about alertly for a few minutes. Suddenly he straightens up, presses and stiffens his tail feathers firmly against the log and lets his wings hang downward with feathers slightly spread and angled slightly forward. Then the wings move apart and backward until they are a moderate distance behind the back, then downward and forward a short distance where they pause for about a second.

This entire cycle is repeated with comparatively long pauses included in at least the next eight cycles. Approximately the next ten cycles contain ever shorter pauses and the wings swing ever faster until from about cycle 20 onward they make a steady blur high in front and far behind. The final dozen cycles slow down, with brief pauses again being noticeable in the last two.

Mr. Thunderwings immediately drops his wings toward his feet and raises his tailfan and the crest feathers of his head for a moment or two in a delightfully pert, attractive conclusion to his performance.

The pauses between the first several beats definitely permit the grouse to hear whether anything unusual or dangerous is at hand. It seems to me that the pauses between beats five and six, and six and seven, longer than some of the previous pauses, are for detecting an overconfident predator. When I made a brief noise during the pauseless portion of a performance, the drummer completed the performance. If I made the noise during the first several beats of another performance, he stopped and never completed it; or he changed from drumming to flight in a split second.

Frame by frame analysis of slow-motion moving pictures proves the drummer swings his wings against nothing but air. The shaping or cupping of the speeding wings simply percussions the air, and may be compared to cracking the whip or to sonic booms. The audible portion of each performance lasts 10 to 12 seconds; and, according to slowed-down tape recordings, contains about 50 beats.

The approximate pattern may be suggested by the following series of dots, words and alphabetical letters. The dots indicate pause length. Where there are no dots, there is no pause. The full

Ruffed grouse drumming, front view . . .

words, shorter wording and alphabetical letters indicate faster and faster beats:

```
Thump . . . . . . . . . . . . . . . . . . . .
thump . . . . . . thump . . . . . . . . . thump
. . . . . . . . thump . . . . . . . . . . thump
. . . . . . . . . . . . . . . thump . . . . . . . .
thump . . . . . . . thump . . . . . . thump
. . . . . . thump . . . . . thump . . . . thump
. . . thump . . . thump . . . thump . . thump
. . thump . . thump . thump . thumpthumpthump
thumpthumpthumpthumpthumpthumpthumpthp
thpthppppppppppthpthpthpthumpthumpthump .
thump . . thump . . . thump!
```

Since the many grouse I have carefully listened to all drum the same way, it appears they follow an inherited pattern implanted at creation.

Drumming proclaims the male's bailiwick and attracts other grouse, especially hens. Upon seeing another grouse, the drummer raises and spreads his attractively patterned tailfan and his sheeny, black ruff to the maximum. He advances in slow motion along his log, but rapidly shakes his head and ruff from time to time. He hisses and pecks the log hard and suddenly rushes off it toward the newcomer. If the newcomer is a bold male, fighting is likely to occur. (A friend of mine saw two grouse fight like farm roosters for 20 minutes. Then they flew with one in hot pursuit of the other.)

If the visitor is a hen, the drummer's belligerent intimidation display changes to solicitation. He contracts his ruff and tailfan, and his tail drags the ground. He even clucks and coos like a hen grouse gathering her chicks (perhaps to suggest motherhood). In due course, sometimes immediately, the courtship is consummated, and the female becomes Mrs. Thunderwings.

The hen must establish a nest on the day of mating at the latest. The nest is a simple, rather round, shallow hollow formed in leaves and duff on the ground usually where there is some overhead protection. Of the eight nests I have seen, two were at the bases of aspen trees surrounded by hazelbrush, one was against the base of a small maple close to a cluster of spreading birch, one was at the base of a small balsam with branches above the nest, one was at the base of a cherry sapling with its broken trunk inclined over the nest, one was against a stump with a long piece of bark extending over the nest, one was against a log also with a long piece of bark extending over the nest (long pieces of bark were scattered around from peeled aspen pulpwood) and one nest was under the root end of an uprooted pine. Five of the eight nests were active when found and known to be between 300 and 1,200 feet of an active drummer. Probably each drummer mated the hen (or hens) in his territory. Hearing a mate's daily drumming possibly assures Mrs. Thunderwings that all is well and encourages her to fill the nest with eggs.

According to research reported in "Of Spring and An Egg," by Jean George, in the April, 1966, *Reader's Digest*, the presence of a male incites the female's development of the egg yolk's final layer. The courtship triggers the passage of the

side view . . .

back view . . .

63

egg into the oviduct. As soon as an egg in the oviduct is fertilized, it moves through stages in which layers of albumen, protective membranes and the outer shell are formed, all in a total of 20½ hours. Hence, one egg is laid each day. Fertilized eggs must be laid and incubated to an internal temperature of 99.5° F. before chick development can begin.

I have not determined if daily mating is required to fertilize each egg; I assume not. Egg laying for northern Wisconsin grouse begins in April and/or early May, depending on the weather. Assuming the laying schedule is normal, Mrs. Thunderwings may lay one egg a day for about 12 days. During that time she does not warm the accumulating eggs enough to start chick development. (Hatching an egg a day may pose many problems.) Once enough eggs are laid, she incubates them for approximately 3½ weeks.

She leaves the nest occasionally to walk about and feed on dewdrop grass, bugs, worms, leaves and the like, all available from handy vegetation.

Ruffed grouse in fantailing display.

Most of the time, however, she sits on the eggs, panting when the sun shines warmly on her and enduring rain in bad weather.

One day I discovered a hen with porcupine quills in the head, the cheek and her lower side. Perhaps a porcupine had wandered too close to the brave mother, and she charged him. With wings beating and bill pecking, she evidently had acquired some of the ever ready quills. Fortunately, in due time she broke the quill on top of her head, and somehow managed to rid herself of all the others.

In late May or early June, the actual hatching occurs. Inside an egg the chick's neck and head are in a position that permit the chick to peck a portion of the shell next to a shoulder. By careful listening, I have heard an occasional faint click-click-click of pecking. When the shell is open enough for part of the chick's head and body to show, the chick expands the opening more by pushing.

Wet, scraggly and floppy, a grouse chick is definitely not able to take off in flight as soon as it is out of the shell. It takes about an hour for the feathers to become fluffy and pretty and for the chick to become active. Often some of the chicks are fully hatched before others start opening their shells.

While the latecomers are still hatching, the first chicks come out from under the mother one or more at a time. They sit beside her, climb on her back, explore the surroundings up to 6 feet from her, peck at grass, leaves and anything else within reach, take catnaps on the ground and work back under her from time to time. Seven chicks are the most I have seen out from under a hen at one time.

During the hours of hatching, Mrs. Thunderwings serenades her family with continual soft, melodious clucking and cooing. She appears at ease and content most of the time, even dozing, but with eyes only half closed. A crack of a stick in the woods, noise in the blind or any passing creature instantly alerts her. Sometimes she may reach her head into the nest and flip out half an egg shell.

After all the little ones are hatched, especially if nothing alarming or disturbing has occurred, the family may remain at the nest several hours more, doubtless to develop strength and ability for their hazard-filled life ahead. For one family I observed, the time from first peep to exodus was 24 hours; for another family it was 36 hours.

When they leave the nest, the hen walks a few yards and clucks and "purrts" quite loudly. Though the chicks have never before heard these sounds, they toddle out of the nest and tag after her, peeping sweetly. Soon the fascinating little family disappears among leafy plants and brush, but never from an observer's heart and memory.

Whenever I chance upon the family later, the chicks scatter according to their fast developing abilities to run or fly. Mrs. Thunderwings rushes close to me, usually once, with tailfan and ruff spread, and she hisses. Then she puts on the well-known broken-wing act, accompanied by whining and whimpering and the "look-I'm-helpless-you-can-catch-me-now"sounds; but she always keeps a few yards beyond reach. When she thinks she has led me far enough, she runs or sneaks or flushes away on thunderous wings. Soon she walks among the dispersed chicks, mothering them back together again. Any chick that really has become separated from the family peeps loudly until the hen finds him. She guards and guides her clutch almost always without help from the male.

In summer, adult grouse make dusting baths on punky dry-rot logs and sandy knolls. Similar to the dusting baths of farm fowl, these are from 8 to 12 inches in diameter and approximately 1½ inches deep. Shaking the dust in and out of their feathers helps them cope with any small insects which bother them. During part of the summer, the adults molt and lose feathers so extensively that they cannot fly. I do not know if the chicks molt, but farm chicks shed feathers; perhaps grouse chicks do, too.

By autumn they all fly quite well, as many a hunter can attest. As often as not, one or several burst from peace and quiet with such startling suddenness that the hunter stands entranced; and, during the flight, this seeming paralysis is intensified by a grouse's ability to keep a large tree trunk or anything else obstructive between himself and the hunter.

Grouse have the unique habit of plunging into deep snow where they spend the night comfortably and completely hidden. In the morning, if nothing has disturbed them, they simply come out a foot or so beyond where they plunged in, and walk to nearby cover, which may be brush or low-limbed evergreens. When I have hiked, snowshoed or skied in grouse country before they came out in the morning, often I have been greatly thrilled to suddenly see a half dozen grouse burst forth from untracked snow into full thunderous flight right before my eyes.

In winter, grouse walk a lot on the snow, making interesting tracks to which they add attractive wing tip patterns when they take off, perhaps to light high in a tree to eat buds. It is a lovely sight to see several grouse standing, stretching and walking far out on limbs silhouetted against a winter evening afterglow.

Sometimes sleet so crusts the snow and coats twigs and buds thick with ice, that many grouse perish. But, come spring, the survivors begin again the marvelous cycle of drumming, courtship, egg laying, egg hatching, chick raising and season adaptings. And, come spring, I am attracted all over again to that mysterious sound emanating from a hidden spot in the deep woods.

Ruffed grouse chick several days old.

The Brown Pelican

By Ernest S. Booth

Photography by W. Daniel Sudia

Brown pelicans are a familiar sight along the waterways of Florida, the Gulf of Mexico and the coasts of California and Oregon. They are among the largest birds in the Western Hemisphere, although slightly smaller than their near relative, the white pelican.

On the docks at St. Petersburg, Florida, one may come near the brown birds, for they are fed by tourists and have become quite tame. A line of them can often be seen flying just beyond the third breaker along any shore, their wings nearly touching the surface of the water.

It is while flying that their graceful motions can most easily be observed.

When a pelican becomes hungry, he begins to fly 20 to 25 feet above the water (sometimes as high as 70 feet), watching intently for fish near the surface. When a likely fish is sighted, he folds his wings and plummets headfirst into the water with his huge beak open. Two or three gallons of water, as well as the fish, are caught in his beak; but the water is not swallowed. The beak forms a fishnet, which is instantly closed after capturing the fish. The bird surfaces quickly, for he has not gone far underwater, and holds his head down while the water drains from his mouth, leaving nothing but the fish. With a toss of his head, the pelican swallows the fish headfirst.

Many people believe that pelicans eat great quantities of valuable fish, and fishermen have long felt it their duty to destroy them. However, biologists have proved that the pelicans actually eat nothing but scrap fish—species not desired by people.

I have visited nesting colonies of the brown pelican in the mangrove swamps of the Florida Keys and found dozens of nests placed four to six feet above the water. By being cautious, it was possible to approach the nesting birds and watch the young. Feeding is a curious process, for the parents have already swallowed and partially digested the fish which they bring to the youngsters. One parent comes to the nest, opens his beak wide with head held down, while junior practically climbs in. The youngster places his beak inside the throat of the adult and helps himself to a meal of fish soup.

Pelicans always nest in colonies where the nests may be placed as near each other as three to five feet. Usually two or three large dull-whitish eggs are laid, which hatch in about a month into some of the ugliest baby birds known. Pelicans of any age are seldom known for their beauty, but they are among the most interesting birds found anywhere.

The WOLVERINE:

BANDIT OF THE NORTHLAND

By Henry N. Ferguson
Photography by Leonard Lee Rue III

Horace McCallum, a 53-year-old Cree Indian, tossed a bundle of pelts onto the counter at the Hudson's Bay Company store at The Pas in Manitoba, Canada. He had just come down from Brochet, 285 air miles north of The Pas, to sell his winter's catch. Included in his bundle were 13 wolverine furs. Horace held the floor

WOLVERINE

as, through an interpreter, he angrily denounced this strange forest creature.

"The wolverine is the biggest nuisance in the north; he is the biggest stealer," shouted Horace. "This year the wolverine destroyed 40 minks on me. They foul my traps." The wolverine, he explained, will follow a trapline looking for baited animals for food. That was what happened to his 40 minks, and the depredations had cost Horace a minimum of $600.

Horace is not alone in his low opinion of this shadowy demon of the North. No less an authority than Ernest Thompson Seton, the famous American naturalist, painted a sinister picture of the wolverine with these words: "Picture a weasel—and most of us can do that—a little demon of destructiveness, that small atom of insensate courage, that symbol of slaughter, sleeplessness, and tireless energy. Picture that scrap of demoniac fury, multiply that mite by 50, and you have a likeness of the wolverine."

Excepting for a few now living in Glacier National Park, the Sequoias and the Sierra Nevadas, the wolverine is a rarity in the United States. Probably there are only a few score within our borders. On the Great Barrens of Canada, in the Yukon Flats and Mount McKinley National Park in Alaska; in upper Scandinavia, Finland and Russia's northern forests, a few still survive, but nowhere in abundance. So elusive is the wolverine that it is likely you can count on the fingers of both hands the number of living men who have glimpsed a live wolverine in the forest.

Alone and unafraid, this creature faces desperate odds against survival, and overcomes them. Unlike a bear, he does not sleep away the long winter. He accumulates no stores of food for the time when blizzards rage across forest and tundra. Withstanding appalling cold or storm, he ranges the northern wilds in a continuous search for food. Incapable of bursts of speed that might capture fleet-footed animals, possessing no special gifts for stalking, handicapped by vision weaker than many other predators, he cruises doggedly through the wilderness, covering immense distances, never missing an opportunity for a snack here, a banquet there, no matter what risks are involved.

The wolverine has a dark brown coat which is ringed by a lighter, yellowish belt that flows from each shoulder, along each side, across each hip and meets at the base of the tail. He has odd yellowish "eyebrows" that form a mask-like marking above the eyes. A powerfully built animal, he has short squat legs, a bushy tail and hair-

covered feet. He is some 3 to 4 feet long, including his tail, weighs 20 to 40 or more pounds, is an exceptionally strong swimmer and can climb trees like a squirrel.

The Eskimos and Indians regard the wolverine, or *le carcajou* as they call him, as a link between their world and the spirit world. When a wolverine is caught, the body is left at least a mile from the village for 5 days. During this time, the spirit of the creature is supposed to leave the body and will not thereafter inflict itself upon a family or pursue a human spirit through eternity.

Because of his small stature, the wolverine hardly qualifies as a candidate for the title of the fiercest creature on earth. Yet, Kodiak bears, the largest flesh-eating animals around today, are afraid of him. He is perfectly capable of defending himself against an entire pack of wolves; and he has been known to pit his strength against a 1,400-pound moose in a life-and-death struggle, and emerge the victor.

Ordinarily, the wolverine is not an aggressive animal, but he will fight desperately when attacked. Regardless of the odds, he will never retreat. "Win or die" is his motto. In battle he has an incredible mixture of strength, ferocity and cunning.

Scientists, trappers and Indians all agree that it's about as safe to enter the den of a mother grizzly as to face a mother wolverine with her young. One of the gentlest and most loving of mothers, she is a tigress in her ferocity when her cubs are in danger. In such cases she is so fearless and savage that even an armed hunter risks his life upon approaching her. She will fight to the end, never yielding an inch. And while the last spark of life remains, she is a raging fury.

Nature has equipped the wolverine well for his role as a fearsome fighter. In battle with an enemy, he is a twisting, slashing blur of sheer fury that bewilders and terrifies an adversary. His teeth are marvelously designed cutting instruments. Angled in such a way that they actually cut like shears, they can slash through a 2-inch-thick rope at a single bite. His claws are 2 inches long, and curved, giving him additional armament.

As a last resort, the wolverine brings into the fray his secondary defense, a musk odor that has no comparison. From a special sac he can release a vile liquid which has a musty, poorly ventilated old cellar smell mixed with a pungency like the odor of rotting meat. It is a potent weapon.

The wolverine has the combined cunning of many generations of criminals. He breaks open caches, raids cabins, systematically destroys everything he encounters and soils food which he cannot eat. He will steal anything he can carry away: pots, pans, clothing, shoes, blankets, books and even small pieces of furniture.

In scores of instances, a solitary wolverine has followed a line of marten traps for 30 miles or more, extracting and devouring the bait or the entrapped victim. He frequently adds insult to injury by hiding the traps, often dropping them through the ice of a frozen stream or lake. The Hudson's Bay Company long ago advised its trappers that they have but two alternatives when a wolverine appears on a trapline: kill the wolverine or seek a new territory.

The creature's feats of strength are legendary. A trapper near Cordova, Alaska, once captured a wolverine and deposited him for safekeeping in a 55-gallon oil drum made of sheet steel. He removed the bung so the animal could get fresh air. During the night, the prisoner wedged its jaws into the bunghole, ripped away the steel until he had an opening large enough to escape.

However you rate the intelligence, the strength, the tenacity, the wildness of mammals, you have to list the wolverine at or near the top in most instances. He is a successful loner; but, as populations explode and remote places succumb to civilization, the loner characteristics of the wolverine will threaten his extinction.

Old CHISELTOOTH:

AMERICA'S LARGEST RODENT

By Leonard E. Foote
Photography by the Author

America is said to be the only country in the world that has nearly exterminated many of its wild creatures and then set about purposely to restore them by law—and been successful at it.

Such is the story of North America's largest rodent, the beaver. When the first European settlers arrived, the animal thrived in large colonies throughout the temperate parts of North America but was most abundant where aspen trees, its favorite food, were plentiful.

In the Adirondack Mountains alone the primitive beaver population is believed to have numbered a million. In 1850, one area 6 by 8 miles on the southwest shore of Lake Superior, west of Marquette, contained 63 dams, 39 lodges and a population of nearly 300 beavers. Small wonder that early trappers found the beaver a source of easy wealth.

North American Indians established the earliest game laws which gave protection to beavers and other animals. But with the western migration of trappers and other pioneers across both the United States and Canada, the animal dwindled slowly in some wilderness areas but disappeared rapidly in others.

Trappers, of course, sought out the spots most densely populated by the animal. Some trappers found it profitable to work in a single area year round. Audubon and Bachman wrote of Rocky Mountain trapping: "A good trapper

beaver and other nearly lost wildlife. By 1910 many states had enacted laws protecting such animals within their boundaries.

After 1900 some beavers in Rutherford Stuyvesant's game preserve in New Jersey escaped and began to spread over parts of the state. Six beavers introduced in the Adirondacks in 1904 had increased to about 150 by 1908, and by 1924 the population numbered more than 5,000. Restocking began in Vermont in 1921 when six beavers were released in Bennington County. Twenty years later, they had been transplanted over most of the state and by 1950 were so abundant that damage became prevalent.

Beaver reappeared in Virginia in 1915, in West Virginia in 1922 and in Kansas in 1924. So successful were the transplants and the protection afforded them that by 1925, more than 250,000 inhabited the United States.

Old **CHISELTOOTH** used to catch about 80 beavers in the autumn, 60 or 70 in the spring and upwards of 300 in the summer in the mountains, occasionally taking as many as 500 in one year."

By 1891 beavers began to get scarce. They were known to be gone from Kansas, Pennsylvania, Virginia, practically extinct in Manitoba and very rare in Maine. Scattered fugitives existed in the remote swamps of the northwest and the Rockies and the impenetrable southern swamps. They were shier than ever before and seldom appeared in daylight. Except for their dams, they might have eluded notice.

So ruthless was the slaughter that by the turn of this century only a few relic beaver colonies remained in the most remote parts of the continent.

But in the early 1900's, Rough Rider Theodore Roosevelt and forester Gifford Pinchot began a successful conservation campaign aimed at protecting

The current North American beaver population is estimated to be several million. The habits of this once almost-liquidated rodent provide a unique wildlife study.

The four, bright-orange incisor teeth of the beaver are his chief tools in the battle for life. The cutting edges of each pair are sharpened against the other. When accidentally broken, they regrow with such rapidity that within a few days they are again chisel-like. Occasionally, a broken tooth will regrow without meeting its opposing member—a condition called malocclusion —and the tooth will finally grow into a great spiral, penetrating the brain or throat and ending in death for the animal.

It is believed that beaver are so skillful that they can always make a tree fall toward the stream. Actually they cut the trees on the bank which lean toward the water first and these do fall streamward. But when cutting farther from the bank, felled trees often fall away from the nearest water and occasionally will lodge in nearby trees. Cottonwoods, tulip poplars and gums which measure up to 3 feet in diameter may be cut, but trees 3 to 8 inches are the usual run. Two beavers can fell a 3-inch sapling in 3 minutes, and a 6-inch tree in an hour or two. The work of felling is usually done by a pair, with assistance at times from their grownup children. In the fall, when an expanding beaver colony is felling trees for winter food storage, a small grove may be reduced in short order. A party of surveyors in the beaver country near Marquette heard 19 tree falls in a single night between 7 o'clock and midnight.

A fallen tree is quickly reduced to short lengths which are stored in the autumn at the bottom of the beaver pond to be dragged later into the lodge for winter food. Other branches may be peeled and the bark eaten on the spot. The peeled branches are then either used in the dam or piled on top of the lodge.

Old CHISELTOOTH

The dam is the most famous and perhaps the most remarkable of the beaver's undertakings. It is a vast structure of sticks, rocks, roots, mud and sod laid across a running stream to back up the water. This insures the beavers enough depth to protect them from enemies all summer, and in the north, to prevent the pond water from freezing to the bottom in winter.

Dams are usually built on small streams, trickles or mere spring runs. Seldom is one attempted on a large, fast-flowing river with a depth greater than 2 feet. First, brush is laid in the deepest part of the stream bed which forms a resistance against the current. As each stick is laid, it is partly covered with rocks, mud or clay to hold it down. This process is carried on until the wall is raised and the original bed of the stream is blocked. As the stream begins to back up, the family works on the dam, piling up sticks and burying them with mud, fibrous roots or anchoring them with rocks of 1 to 6 pounds in weight. Mud is dug from the pond immediately above the dam making it the deepest area of the pond.

A beaver lodge is often built nearby. Often it is formed from an old bank burrow used by the beaver when the stream was free-running. Bank burrows are the homes of exploring beaver, usually second-year young, driven from the parents when a new litter arrives each summer. As the water rises, the dry chamber in the bank burrow becomes flooded; and the animals begin piling peeled food sticks on top of the old burrow. They dig upward so that, as the dam is raised, the lodge expands, always with a dry, above-water interior chamber. Here the beavers loaf during the day, and here the young are born in a chamber lined with shredded bark or corn shucks, if the latter is handy.

Beavers mate during midwinter, usually in late January or early February. After about 3 months, 2 to 8 young are born. The young kits are remarkably well developed at birth, with well-furred bodies and open eyes. They remain in the lodge for about a month, then leave to swim and find solid food. Weaning is completed in about 6 weeks, and by fall the young are actively engaged in food gathering, dam repair and other activities of the colony. They continue to live in the lodge until a new litter is born the following year.

When high waters threaten to flood the dark nursery in the lodge, adult beavers hastily enlarge the ventilation hole and deposit the young in a makeshift nest atop the lodge. Here they loaf and bask, sleep and play in the warm sun until the water goes down. After a nap, the kits may slip down a muddy side of the lodge for a refreshing dip in the chocolate-colored water or climb around on the piled alders, poplars and gums for a better look at the community life passing by in the flood waters.

The young are so well-furred that the air trapped in the thick layer of underhair makes diving a trick to be learned. Little beavers are diminutive images of their 60-pound parents, with valved ears that automatically close to shut out water, webbed hind feet and trowel-like tail. At this tender age, little beavers haven't yet learned that they are destined to be both water conservationists and dam nuisances.

As little beavers mature, they take longer swimming trips from their lodge, and eventually become an integral part of the unusual environment they create, maintain and help populate. A beaver pond is a strange and fascinating place. In it, wood ducks swim their broods; and water snakes, banded with hammered copper, vent their disagreeable dispositions on anything, large or small, that disturbs their sunbathing.

Late spring in a beaver pond is a noisy time. Spring peeper frogs begin a singing cadence of soprano calls in the night; and, later, bullfrogs add their bass to the din. During daylight hours the swamp rings with the grunting "chuck" call of the king rail, the screeching song of the male redwing blackbird and the sonorous croak of the green heron. The swamp water ripples with swarms of top minnows, a basic item in the diets of monstrous swamp bass and every other nonvegetarian inhabiting the flowage.

Capitalizing on the stable water level, muskrats move in to compete with the beavers for summer's succulent water weeds and to build ostentatious feeding platforms of vegetable delicacies in the rushes or along the muddy shore. This entire community is dependent upon the beaver colony and its engineering works for fresh water, and its plant and animal successions are essential to the lives of all of them.

Spring floods are slowed down by beaver dams. Some of the impounded water percolates into the ground and runs out months later as artesian aquifers, flowing springs or into farmers' wells. Most of the water which goes over the dam has been held up in the pond until the flood has passed on. This helps to maintain an even flow to generate electricity at electric power plants and to float boats and barges in navigable channels further downstream.

For a beaver colony to thrive, dams must be raised periodically to flood new timber, especially tulip poplars, willows and gums. If some of this new ground happens to include a cornfield, or if the damsite coincides with a railway or highway culvert, then the beaver colony, farmer, highway engineer and state game commission are all in for trouble. To the beavers, corn is good food, the stalks are just the thing to trim the inside of a new lodge, and a culvert is the best damsite man ever gave to an expanding colony.

So there are conflicts between beavers and farmers seeking to grow corn, agricultural engineers draining wet land for pasture, highway builders and tree farmers. Often the conflicts can be compromised by installing perforated drainage pipes in the beaver dams or a solid drainage pipe which penetrates the dam and extends well into the pond upstream. These devices must be a source of frustration to the beaver colony, for they cannot usually be plugged, and man can maintain the water level to prevent further flooding.

Beavers are industrious and beneficial to their environment and continually show cause for their status among nature's other wildlife.

The Beesleys and Their Woodland

By Bill Thomas

From the beginning, there was a certain kind of harmony — something like a sixth sense — between the Beesleys of Cedar Grove and nature's children. They have no children of their own, but Lloyd and Adele have a special feeling toward the animals, the birds and the flowers that grow wild in these wooded hills of southeastern Indiana. And apparently these inhabitants of the forest sense that feeling, too, for they gather here like orphans yearning for kindness, begging for understanding.

Farmers they are by trade, but the rolling 160-acre hill farm produces more than livestock and hay crops. It produces warblers and mockingbirds, wild ducks, skunks, rabbits, hummingbirds, red-tailed hawks and buzzards, raccoons and opossums. They are not here in spectacular numbers, but you can wander into the woods almost any time and see some wildlife.

On the back side of the Beesley farm is a glacial woodland, and here the wild flowers grow in such great abundance that it would take years to photograph all of the different species. Lloyd and Adele have taken up this hobby, and already they have spent twenty-five years photographing the wild flowers of their forest. Neither of the Beesleys has more than an eighth-grade formal education, but

Lloyd Beesley's rapport with the wild creatures which frequent his farm area is displayed as he rubs noses with his wild pet cottontail, Robert.

once a year they are invited to lecture to the Indiana Academy of Science. Here they speak before Ph. D's, some of whom are experts on wild flowers themselves.

The Beesleys have photographed in intricate detail more than five hundred species of wild flowers right around their home. Each year they continue to add to their slide collection, locating a new species every now and then.

Luck smiled on the Beesleys from the outset. Lloyd and Adele were both young when they first became interested in wild flowers. There were always plenty of them around, some extremely rare. And it was because of the glacial soil of the woodland that they grew there.

Growing in abundance, for instance, on the Beesley farm is the Indian paintbrush, a wild flower native to the Montana and Wyoming area. Many tiny lichens, some not yet named, grow here, too, indicating perhaps that they may not be found in any other part of the country — or the world.

The Beesleys spend many hours getting into position and waiting for the most ideal conditions to photograph wild flowers. A slight breeze — ever so noticeable — is enough to set a bloom in motion. Lloyd takes no chances on a blur. He wants a top quality photograph, and that is what he ultimately gets.

The Beesleys had no plans of ever doing anything with their wild flower slides; they were collecting them for personal enjoyment. When people in the neighborhood heard about the collection, however, they were soon asked to lecture and show their slides before PTA groups and womens' clubs in Franklin and adjoining counties. Their reputation spread.

In 1964, Marian College at Indianapolis invited them to lecture. And the following spring they were asked for the first time to show their slides and lecture at the Indiana Academy of Science, meeting that year at Culver Military Academy in Culver, Indiana. Since then, they have been on the program annually.

"These were botanists and biologists representing almost every field," explained Adele, a note of soft pride in her voice. "And yet they were amazed that we had photographed so many different kinds of wild flowers. In fact, they couldn't believe some of these even exist in this part of the country . . . and according to some of the established authorities on the subject, they really don't."

Not all of the wild flowers they photograph are from southeastern Indiana, for they carry their camera equipment wherever they go. When they honeymooned in the Ozarks a few years ago, they photographed wild flowers, and they have photographed them in Ohio, Kentucky and Tennessee.

The Beesleys love country life, and their simple, two-story frame house sits nearly a mile off the closest major road, well isolated from civilization. A wide array of friends ranging from authors, scientists and teachers to common laborers and factory workers visit frequently, for they too have found this a delightful retreat. The yard borders on two small spring-fed lakes in which abound bluegill, largemouth bass, white crappie and catfish. Wild ducks stop to mingle with the domestic ducks kept on the farm. Sometimes they spend the winter and the Beesleys feed them along with the rest. One pair of ducks decided to make this their permanent home and last summer they raised their young.

A chipmunk romps in a large cage in the dining room of the Beesley home; a quail, found abandoned when it was a chick, shares a curtain rod perch in the bathroom with a rose-breasted grosbeak which was found injured beside the highway. The Beesleys took the bird to the veterinarian who

Many birds nest on the Beesley acreage. One summer a pair of wild ducks nested here, and Lloyd and Adele enjoyed helping the parent ducks raise the young ones.

helped them nurse it back to health. Now neither bird wants to leave the Beesley home. It is the same way with Robert, a wild cottontail that sleeps under Lloyd's bed and occasionally hops up to nuzzle him or to tickle his nose with its whiskers during the night. Raccoons, opossums, turtles and even skunks have been visitors at various times in the Beesley home. And all were more than welcome.

A couple of years ago, friends of the Beesleys brought them two tiny raccoons whose mother had been killed. The babies were shy at first and would not eat for several days, but then their fears were overcome. They began to take bread dipped in milk. The milk and bread diet lasted a few days, and then they ate in earnest — apples, nuts, potato chips, candy, corn on the cob, watermelon, fish and fried chicken.

"With such a menu, how could they help but like us," laughed Adele.

Within ten days, the Beesleys were handling their new friends without gloves and without fear of being either scratched or bitten. The raccoons and the Beesleys had already congealed a rapport that dispelled all fears.

It was a little different the day Lloyd was mowing hay and came upon a litter of little skunks. Dismounting from the tractor, he picked up the babies to move them aside so the mower would not harm them. The little ones did not try to spray their aroma on him, but Lloyd had not counted on the mother skunk. She seemingly came from nowhere and . . . well . . . it was several minutes before Lloyd could see at all. He had already shouted for Adele to bring the camera. She came rushing up just in time to get a good squirt of the scent herself. Both roamed helplessly in the hayfield, blind as bats and carrying four baby skunks by their tails with an uneasy mother near by.

"Somehow we got pictures of those little rascals," recalled Lloyd, "but I'll never know just how."

Many of the animals and birds that have become pets of the Beesleys while being reared or nursed back to health now have returned to the wilds. But some of them still live in the neighborhood, such as the two raccoons, long since full grown. In winter, when foraging for food becomes a real problem during the heavy snows, they come to the back door of the Beesley home and Adele gives them food. When the snows leave, it may be a year before they are seen again.

Although both Lloyd and Adele grew up in the hills overlooking the small village of Cedar Grove and the magnificent Whitewater River Valley, it was quite a twist of fate that led Lloyd to stay on the farm. When he was a teenage boy, he developed a great pitching arm and a tricky knuckleball with the local baseball team. He was so good, in fact, that he went to Florida for spring training with the Boston Red Sox. That was back in 1936.

The same spring, the late Charlie Dressen, then manager of the Cincinnati Reds, approached him to try out for that team. He was about to do just that when his father became seriously ill. His mother, now aged and nearly blind, could neither care for herself nor Lloyd's father. Lloyd gave up his dreams of a baseball career and returned home to stay. Although he has often wondered what his life might have been like had he signed a contract with either the Reds or the Red Sox, he has never regretted his return to the farm.

After all, it would have been mighty hard to make friends with a wild rabbit named Robert or a wild duck named Sam in pro baseball.

The variety of flowering plants in Indiana woodlands brings scholars and educators from many states and universities. This brilliant fire pink, Silene virginica, *is not too common but can be found by carefully searching.*

*Early glaciers brought the seeds of hundreds of
wild flowers to the glaciated soil of the Beesley farm.
They have discovered many extremely rare species,
one of these being the Phlox pilosa.*

Photo by Lloyd Beesley

Photo by Lloyd Beesley

ADVENTURES O

By Tom Wilson

Drawings by Joe Maniscalco

It was mid-afternoon—a warm, sunny, windless day. Rollo, the sea otter, was indulging in his favorite sport, riding the sea waves as a surfer would. He would latch onto a giant wave, lower his tail and legs and sail toward shore. Just before the wave would break for its final assault onto the beach, Rollo would execute a complete graceful somersault under water and head back out to sea. He didn't venture out very far, just past the breakers. His arch enemies were always waiting for him farther out, past the kelp beds. The only sea creatures he was afraid of were sharks and blue whales. Only one other enemy disturbed him and that was man. In days gone by, man had exploited his breed for the most sought-after and rarest fur in the world. The Russians had practically decimated the sea otter population in a 170-year quest for fur. Now the sea otter were protected by law. They didn't know this, so they were constantly wary of man. Rollo's sensitive ears could pick up the sound of man's voice even above the pounding of the surf.

After an hour or so of surfing, Rollo tired and sought relaxation in the kelp beds. Before going to sleep, Rollo wrapped strands of kelp around his body to keep waves from washing him ashore. Rollo had never been to shore and never intended to go. He rolled over on his back and stuck his tail and two hind legs straight up in the air. With one of his forelegs he covered his eyes against the sun and was rocked to sleep by the gentle rollers.

When Rollo awoke, he was hungry. He unwrapped himself and dived to the bottom in search of food. It was no problem, really. His diet was simple. He never ate fish; he existed on sea urchins, crabs and other crustaceans. His favorite meal was abalone; crab meat was almost as good. Since Rollo's teeth were somewhat like human teeth—sharp in front, flat in back with rounded edges—he couldn't crack sea shells with them. While he was on the forage for food, he would pick up a stone and bring it to the surface with him. Then he would lie on his back, place the stone on his chest and with his forefeet he would smash the crab or other shellfish against the stone until he could separate the meat. Then he would clutch the meat in both forepaws and roll over and over to wash any shell particles from it. He would eat leisurely and daintily, similar to a human. He was extremely fastidious.

As his territory Rollo had chosen a stretch of the ocean from Jenner by the Sea to Fort Ross. There were ample kelp beds along the route, and sharks would never venture into them.

Rollo was lonesome for the company of other otter, but their presence was rare. Occasionally he would go on a hunt for some of his kind to sport with, but the only ones he could find were older married males or mothers cuddling their young. Rollo could remember his mother cradling him in one foreleg for hours on end when he was a pup. Later on, when he was a cub, his mother taught him the dangers of life and how to find and prepare food. Rollo's father was always near but took no part in his upbringing. After a year passed, Rollo's mother made it clear that he was on his own. Her job was finished. She and his father vanished from his life, and he never saw them again.

Now Rollo was 2 years old, not quite fully grown, but 4 feet long and weighing 60 pounds. When he moved through the water, it was with

ADVENTURES OF ROLLO

MANISCALCO

the stimulus of the stormy seas and mated and honeymooned. The mating was natural and unaffected, instigated by either one or both.

When they finally reached the breakers off the Jenner coast, they settled down to a life of rollicking fun and laziness. Food was plentiful and neither man nor sharks bothered them. Life was complete, almost.

When the pup was born in the springtime, Rollo's mate apparently deserted him. She spent all of her time on the surface, cuddling the little one in her forelegs. She lay on her back and nursed him. The only time she left the baby was when she dived for food. She would tie him in the kelp before she left. Rollo would follow her to the bottom, but she never gave him a tumble. Rollo was alone again. Funtime was over.

As it had been with his father, Rollo had no part in raising his offspring. His mate knew he was there and took comfort and courage in the knowledge of his presence, but she didn't outwardly acknowledge his existence. Still Rollo hung around and waited. He had no place else to go.

The pup grew into a cub. Rollo's mate began to wander farther and farther away from the young one, and she stayed away for longer periods of time. Rollo followed everywhere she

more of a gliding movement than swimming. His was a superb illustration of motion. His fur had reached its peak of ultra beauty. It was an inch thick and in two layers. The outer area was brown sprinkled with long silvery white hairs. The inner fur was golden to light brown. When Rollo dived for food, his dense fur would trap a blanket of air and insulate him from the cold of the depths.

Summer finally passed and rough weather set in. Storms were frequent and the water churned and roiled. Rough water seems to make sea otters fidgety, and Rollo became restless. He decided to search for a mate, but that wasn't easy to accomplish. Whether it was instinct that guided him or something that his mother had told him, he didn't know; but he headed for the coast of Monterey. The roaring seas tired him easily, and he rested often; but his hunger was minimal.

On his fifth day of fighting strong ocean currents, he headed for a kelp bed just off the coast of Santa Cruz to take a snooze. There among the bladders of floating kelp he saw her. She rolled over from her position of repose and greeted him. Then and there began instantaneous friendship and companionship. There was no shyness or preliminaries. He had found his wife mate. They splashed, rolled, dived, rode the waves together, had fun and were contented. Rollo started to eat again. In fact, he ate as much as one-third his weight each day in sea urchins.

Together they headed back north to Rollo's home territory. On the way, they succumbed to

went. One day Rollo's mate simply didn't bother to return to the cub. She had taught him all she knew.

Immediately the old friendship and companionship returned between Rollo and his mate. They played together as before. Life was truly complete. They belonged to each other again.

NATURE'S MASTER EXCAVATOR

By Russell Tinsley

From the Outdoor
Photographers League

I came upon the drama while walking amid a grassy plain of central New Mexico a few years ago. I stood motionless and watched a coyote, belly laid low, sneaking through the grass toward two prairie dogs playfully cavorting around their ground burrows on an open knoll.

All the suspense of nature's survival was in the coyote's stalk. He would take a few quick, quiet steps, then lie down and eye the small

MASTER EXCAVATOR

creatures. For several minutes the predator remained absolutely motionless, slipping forward only when the prairie dogs looked in another direction. The insidious coyote crept still closer and sank behind a clump of grass, waiting impatiently, his muscles tensed.

Suddenly, he sprang. But it took only a split second for the alert and nimble prairie dogs to realize their danger and pile into their burrows. All the hungry coyote got for his trouble was dust. He paused and peered at the holes in the ground. Then turning, he trotted off.

Shortly after the coyote left, tiny heads began to pop up from seemingly every ground burrow in sight. It wasn't long before the prairie dogs emerged and began running around again, as if nothing had happened to interrupt them.

Prairie dogs are accustomed to such shenanigans. This diminutive inhabitant of the plains—built close to the ground and averaging about 14 to 16 inches in length and two to three pounds in weight—is a constant target of carnivorous creatures, especially coyotes, badgers, hawks, owls, eagles and bobcats. But despite this incessant threat, the prairie dog, with his lightning reflexes and swift speed for his build and size, has more than held his own except for one predator—man. Humans with poison have accomplished what nature has been unable to do—check the rapidly multiplying animal.

The prairie dog is indigenous to this country. Actually, the name is a misnomer. Though he does resemble a small puppy, he is in no way related. He is a member of the squirrel family. Lewis and Clark wrote of a "barking squirrel that lives in ground burrows." The Indians called him "wishtonwish," so named because of the characteristic shrill whistle, much like that of the marmot, a cousin. Whether the common name was derived from the chirp or bark or the puppy-like appearance, no one knows.

Prairie dogs were once quite common on the Great Plains. The gregarious animals built "towns" which stretched for miles and were composed of thousands of burrows. Naturalist Vernon Bailey wrote about one town in northern Texas that, at the turn of the century, covered an area roughly 100 miles wide and 250 miles long, with an estimated population of 400 million inhabitants.

Prairie dogs are amazingly efficient excavators. When they get their minds on digging, the front claws become a blur of motion as they "bite" into the soil and heap it up behind them. A burrow can be detected by this telltale mound at the entrance. A typical burrow is about three to four inches in diameter at the mouth and angles down for several feet before leveling off. It isn't unusual for one to go almost straight down for perhaps ten feet before flattening parallel to the ground surface and running for ten more feet. Multiply this by 100 burrows to get an idea of the subsurface destruction that prairie dogs can create.

But the animal's excavating skill has proved to be his undoing. One prairie dog digging burrows isn't bad; even two are tolerable. But when they reach several dozen in number, the damage

Two young prairie dogs play near their ground burrow.
Photo by William A. Bake

A litter of prairie dogs, usually three or four, stays with the parents several
months before leaving the home burrow.

Photo by Leonard Lee Rue III

can become costly to farmers and ranchers in the area where these creatures live.

I once knew a farmer in north Texas who almost went mad trying to thwart the energetic animals. He irrigated his garden by skirting it with a deep ditch. Ordinarily, the water ran down to the channel and was siphoned off into individual rows. One season the farmer started pumping water into the ditch, but it flowed for a distance and then vanished. Prairie dogs had undermined the garden with such a crisscrossing network of burrows that the water simply drained underground.

The farmer tried adding dirt to plug the hole in the ditch. But the dogs dug faster than he could shovel. He appealed to the county agent who recommended poisoning the pests. This was attempted, but enough escaped to maintain the problem. Finally, the farmer lined the ditch with concrete. This solved the dilemma for a year, but the following spring when he turned on the water an entire section of the ditch gave way. A burrow beneath the concrete had weakened the structure and water pressure broke it through.

The animal also has an enormous appetite for his size, which makes him no less popular with farmers and ranchers. They love fresh field-grown grain, if it is available; but otherwise they dine chiefly on grasses and grass seeds. Insects comprise only about one percent of their total intake. They don't have to drink water because of the large amount of moisture in green plants, roots and grains they eat. Unlike their cousins in the squirrel family, they seldom store food for the winter.

They are predominantly day creatures, feeding in early morning or evening, but often they do sleep at noon in the cool of their underground homes. They never stray far from home. If their nearby food supply diminishes, they simply relocate their burrows. The defenseless prairie dog has no protection except to scamper out of sight. When wandering from his burrow, he is constantly on the lookout for danger. As soon as he sights something suspicious, he emits a high-pitched whistle; and immediately all nearby prairie dogs scoot for their burrows. For awhile they hang around the entrances as though puzzled at what had alarmed them. They don't go completely underground until danger is imminent. Usually they don't stay down long but continue to come up to look around. Such curiosity has proved a prairie dog's downfall more than once.

Mother prairie dogs bear their offspring during April, May or June, depending on the exact locale. They have one litter yearly, usually three or four in number. The young are born blind, hairless and feeble. They weigh about one ounce apiece. By the third week, they have a fine sprinkling of hair, but are fully covered with a soft coat by the fifth or sixth week. Their eyes open about 35 days after birth, and the young make their first appearance above ground at about six weeks of age. The family usually sticks together for several weeks longer, but then the youngsters strike off on their own to set up housekeeping in a nearby abandoned burrow.

Though their present population is only a fraction of what it once was, there is no widespread concern for the prairie dog. He will survive. In fact, his nonhuman enemies—badgers, coyotes, bobcats and other predators—are disappearing in the wild much faster than he is.

Creatures
of the Night

By Jean George
Photographs by Al Staffan

*This young milk snake (Lampropeltis triangulum) is a member of
a species that is economically valuable because of the high proportion of mice
and other small rodent pests it consumes.*

On the sunny afternoon of last June 11 a group of distinguished scientists, publishers and businessmen gathered at the Bronx Zoo in New York City with more than the usual curiosity of zoo-goers. They had come to see the opening of the World of Darkness, the newest and most elaborate of the many exhibits of night creatures that are drawing crowds to zoos all over the United States and Europe. The guests stayed on and on that afternoon, as have the thousands of people that have crowded into the exhibit since. When they left, their concepts of the night and of the animals that inhabit it had been changed forever. Says William G. Conway, General Director of the Bronx Zoological Society, "Two thirds of all the world mammals are nocturnal. Now that we can observe them in action, we know how much we've been missing all these years. World of Darkness is the most popular thing we've ever done."

Edward Maruska, Director of the Cincinnati Zoo, echoes this sentiment. "Our night exhibit has had such fantastic attendance that we are planning to expand into a larger building with more animals and scenery." Zoos in Milwaukee, Wisconsin, and Houston, Texas, report similar successes, as have a number of zoos in England and on the Continent.

The night, to the first-time visitor, is full of surprises. First, it is noisy. As you enter the front half of the World of Darkness exhibit, you are greeted by amplified tape recordings of night hootings and whistlings. The place reverberates with the bellow of bull alligators, the calls of coyotes and frogs. For the first time you'll hear the voices of bats, their ultrasonic calls lowered to the range of the human ear by an electronic device called a "bat translator." The effect has aptly been compared to New York's Times Square when all the theaters are letting out.

Creatures

The animals themselves make for surprises. The young fox at play bounces and cavorts, leaps into the air and richochets off rocks like a four-legged ballerina. The armadillo, inert as a stone by day, comes on jazzy and bright-eyed, striding around a mock-up desert with an exploratory interest in all crannies and ground crevices.

It is the bats, however, that make the deepest impression. Seen in their true environment, they appear not spooky or threatening, but humorous. The little fish bats fly with the unpredictableness of paper airplanes, on wings especially designed for graceful, direct flight, unobstructed and close to the water. But they lack the agile flexibility that some other bat species possess. They squabble with one another, and fight for the best footholds on the walls as they alight. The effect is of many gay, noisy creatures filling the night with ultrasonic racket as they dip and dive for their food.

Zoo directors have long known that the best animal "shows" go on at night. Through the years, many zoos have attempted to reverse the wake-sleep cycle of small animals, hoping to induce nighttime activity during daylight hours. Some experimented with dim blue light, to simulate moonlight, but these experiments had little success because visitors could not see the animals clearly enough. Nevertheless, they came to see what they could, which was an encouraging indication of interest, and more zoos adopted the technique. The Chicago-Brookfield and the Bristol and London Zoos in England displayed kinkajous, gerboas and other nocturnal animals by day—again with less than total success, because of the necessarily dim lighting.

Finally, in 1961, Joseph Davis, now Scientific Assistant to the Director of the Bronx Zoo, reversed a small bush baby, a nocturnal monkey-like primate, with white light at night and bright red lights by day. Nocturnal animals, biologists had discovered, do not see red light. It does not contract the irises as most other lights do.

"She was sensational!" Davis says. "I had always thought of bush babies as shy and dull. She showed me that at night they are as curious and active as diurnal monkeys are by day."

That same year the Bronx Zoo opened an exhibit of small mammals under red light. It also plunged ahead with plans for World of Darkness, an en-

The screech owl
forages for food
at night.

Eastern Harvest Mouse

Creatures

vironmental exhibit in which complete ecological settings—desert, swamps and forests—are vividly reproduced in the minutest detail (acorns on trees, streams running through jungles and woods). New twists were worked out in the lighting, adjusting the colors to fit the needs of the various animals. The *people* are under red lights, the animals move in pure red light or soft, low-intensity white, blue or green light, more pleasant to human eyes than red and yet not obtrusive to the night animals.

Davis and other zoo people are often asked: What *is* a night animal? How did it get that way?

The kingdom of beasts roughly breaks down into four general categories: those most active

Flying Squirrel

by day (diurnal), by night (nocturnal), in twilight hours (crepuscular) and a few opportunists who work both day and night shifts intermittently (arythmic). The division probably started when certain preyed-upon creatures learned to feed and move about in the dark, a safer and less-crowded environment than daytime.

But times and conditions change. Today, anyone who stands outdoors in the dark, listening to the forest, knows that more goes on by night than by day. And in the darkness, many mammals, birds and reptiles find their way about through senses and abilities baffling even to scientists.

The eyes of the more highly developed denizens of darkness, for instance, contain a plethora

Creatures

of "rods"—nerve cells that are ultrasensitive to light—and millions of cells in the retina that magnify light from the moon and stars. (Their reflector cells are what make the animal's eyes glow in automobile headlights). Experiments by Professor Lee R. Dice, at the University of Michigan, have indicated that owls can see a white mouse on dark soil in what was probably less than one millionth of a foot candlepower of light.

Eyes are one of the fascinations of the zoo exhibits; in the dark, the pupils dilate completely, changing the animal's appearance. The cats, foxes, owls and raccoons, yellow-eyed by day, take on a sultry beauty with their eyes of deep, limpid black. The feeling is that one has never really known these creatures before.

In the nighttime jungles of Sumatra, the female red flying frog climbs along a tree limb to locate a small puddle of water beneath her no bigger than a dinner plate and often as far as twelve feet below. "When she is directly over one of these isolated pools," says Bronx Zoo herpetologist Wayne King, "she lays her foamy egg mass on the limb and departs. The tadpoles, upon hatching, fall into the water below. If they miss, they dry up and die. But so keen is this water-locating sense of the frogs in the dark that they almost never miss."

Many snakes and lizards, in darting around, use a sense that is a combination of taste and smell. Forked tongues flashing from their mouths pick up particles of dust, gas and chemicals and insert them into two depressions in the roof of their mouths. The organs guide the animals through the darkness with unerring accuracy as they quite literally follow the "flavors" of the night.

All the pit vipers, including rattlesnakes and copperheads, can "see" heat in the dark. Two pits in the snake's head contain cells that record the heat which all warm-blooded animals emit. Using these cells, the snake can actually focus on the source of heat much as our eyes focus on objects. And certain species have such depth perception with this "sight" that they are able to strike in the dark with the accuracy of a hawk in the daytime.

The night is not all serious pursuit and killing. Courtships in the night are also intriguing.

The male web-weaver spider woos the female in her web with a series of tugs and tweaks on her lines. If she does not signal acceptance, he drops to the ground and dashes away before she tries to eat him. Male American toads leap vigorously on any toad that moves nearby. If the jumped-on toad croaks and shudders, the jumper departs, for only male toads object when seized. Silence indicates to the jumper that he has found a female, and new life begins.

Much of the time after dark is spent in play. A pair of young badgers at the Bronx Zoo can be seen in their look-in den wrestling each other. Two tundra owls on exhibit run along limbs like kittens, hop from tree to rocks and snag leaves with their feet. The bush babies cluster together and groom each other, or run through the trees in gangs. When tired, they nap together in a great heap.

Bat enthusiast Harley B. Sherman, former professor at the University of Florida, came up with the astonishing information that the bats had an organized baby-sitter service. "When darkness comes," he said, "the females hang their babies in a cluster on a wall and take off to hunt food. But one or two adults always stay behind to watch over the infants!"

Rudolf Schenkel, of the Department of Zoology, University of Basel, Switzerland, found that lions in Kenya's Nairobi National Park learn their relative positions of dominance in the pride by testing their strength in sham night battles. Mother lions teach in the dark. A lioness in Schenkel's three-year field study regularly led her cubs out at night to instruct them in responses to other animals—and automobiles! "They closely run beside a slowly rolling car," Schenkel said, "watching the wheels and sometimes striking out at them with a pawing movement." They quickly learned not to chase rolling wheels but things that flee, like wildebeest. Schenkel also observed cubs climbing trees, balancing on fallen logs and playing with water —pawing at it, splashing it and running with its current—a playful way of learning about their environment.

Just as the night is being rolled back by zoo-goers, so is it for many suburban homeowners. Some people put red bulbs in floodlights in their yards and watch deer, raccoons and flying squirrels after dark. Last summer I sat one very still evening, in a neighbor's garden under a red light and watched a doe and her fawn cropping grass within ten feet of me. A raccoon passed within inches of my feet, head down, nose twitching, as he made his way to the garbage can.

Raccoons are great favorites with night nature watchers. A boy on Long Island, New York, puts a simple red bulb in his desk lamp and places it in his first floor window. Every night a neighborhood raccoon comes up a plank from the ground to the window and sits on the sill eating peanuts and apples. A group of boys in Chappaqua, New York, put red cellophane over flashlights to watch spiders spin webs at night and crickets find offerings of bread through their odor-sensitive antennae.

But to me the flying squirrels are the most exciting of all. A very common animal, they are so night-bound that they rarely see human beings. For this reason, a mammalogist told me, they are unafraid of man and can be approached quite closely. I tested this that night in my neighbor's garden when, with a soft thud, one of these beautiful squirrels landed on the bird-feeding station. Moving slowly in the red light, I not only approached the flying squirrel but was able to slide my hand under it. The squirrel wrapped his tail around his soft body and peered up at me with as much curiosity as I looked at him. Then he walked off my fingers and went back to his sunflower seed. For that one moment, the magic of the night's creatures was mine.

Wolf Spider

After "cooling off" a little, this whiptail lizard posed most obligingly for his portrait.

LIZARDS
IN HIS REFRIGERATOR

By Richard H. Utt

When you step into Warren Petersen's apartment in San Jose, California, you can't be sure just what sort of pets you'll meet. Skunks maybe, or a raccoon or a ringtail. Or it could be an owl, a batch of cecropia moths, snakes or lizards. Petersen has domesticated them all at one time or another, and photographed them. To him, wild creatures are not game to shoot, or merely biology specimens to study. They are his photographer's models and, above all, his friends, each with a fascinating, humorous, almost human personality.

The first time I visited Petersen, after he had projected some of his nature slides, he suddenly

start. She was tame and friendly, and quite content to sit in my palm.

"Another name for that kind is the Tenaya lizard," he informed me. "They give birth to live young. In fact, Dinah had five babies last October right here in the house."

I nodded in acknowledging these facts of life. After all, I hadn't expected him to take the expectant lizard to a hospital for confinement.

He patted Lizzie, the other lizard. "This is a coast alligator lizard," he said. "She is oviparous—she lays eggs. Dinah is viviparous; her babies are born live, not as eggs."

As we sat petting our reptiles, making lizard talk, Petersen asked, "Do you know which lizard is the biggest in the country?"

"I've heard it's the Gila monster," I said. "I've seen a couple of them in captivity, but never out on the desert."

"I used to teach at the Apache Indian Agency," my host continued. "That's at San Carlos, Arizona, near Globe. In the spring I'd take my camera on weekends and go out where the cacti were blooming and find some nice plants. I'd dig them up and carry them to my car. Once I saw an extra nice barrel cactus that weighed about 35 pounds. I got it onto my back with a board underneath, hauled it down from the hills and planted it near where we lived.

"Then one afternoon as my wife and I were looking for flowering cacti, hiking over the hills and rolling country, we suddenly came across a Gila monster crawling along the sand. Like all proper Gila monsters he was pudgy and not very fast, and he looked like Indian beadwork all over. Of course, I had heard these fellows are poisonous, and I wasn't going to take chances. I watched him cautiously at first, then moved in a little closer. I found a stick and used it to push him away from a cactus plant that he wanted to crawl under. He moved so slowly that I soon quit worrying about being bitten, though I kept

Dinah, the Sierra alligator lizard, bore five live young while living in Warren Petersen's home.

asked, "Would you like to see my pets?"

"Of course," I answered. What else could I say?

I hadn't the slightest idea what sort of wildlife was sharing his home at the moment. What would it be now? Bears? Butterflies? Porcupines?

He left the room and returned with two lizards, which he introduced to me. "This is Dinah and this is Lizzie. Here, you can hold her." He held out Dinah, a Sierra alligator lizard.

I hadn't cuddled any lizards for a number of years, though as a boy I had caught them using limp stalks of grass with slipknot loops at the ends. But Dinah and I got along fine from the

LIZARDS
IN HIS REFRIGERATOR

Lizzie, the coast alligator lizard, crunches down her dinner of fresh Jerusalem cricket.

my fingers away from his mouth. He looked a little dangerous, too, because he kept sticking out his tongue like a snake does.

"As we followed him, we came across an old 5-gallon milk can that somebody had dumped in the desert along with other trash. I picked it up and prodded my pudgy new friend with the stick till he walked right into the milk can. Then we took him home.

"We put him in the backyard, out by the fence which we made of a crate and some boxes. I had heard these critters like to eat eggs, so I gave him eggs in a dish. He ate them with relish."

"After a couple of weeks I gave him to somebody who wanted to keep him in one of the state parks."

"You have a lot of sharp pictures of lizards taken from just a few inches away," I observed. "How do you keep them from darting under a bush or down a hole somewhere before you can snap the shutter?"

"Usually when you try to shoot pictures of lizards, frogs, toads or even butterflies or other insects, they want to run, jump or fly away. Even when you catch them first, you put them down and they're gone. So I devised a plan, and it works very well. Lizards and these other characters are cold blooded, and the colder they feel, the more sluggish they get. So you put them in the refrigerator, even in the freezer part."

"Isn't that kind of hard on lizards?"

"No, you don't leave them in there very long. Just as soon as they get real cool, you take them out and they are easy to manage. You place them exactly where you want them, with the right background for the picture. They will stay there, and they will keep their feet just so. They will hold their tails in a graceful position, and you can turn their heads toward your camera lens. They will stay posed while you shoot away."

I returned Dinah to her owner who made this final observation: "Sometimes they almost smile for their portraits; and, if you have some imagination, you'll notice that they seem to be saying, 'cheese!'"

Sierra alligator lizard

WHY I SHOOT INSECTS

By Ron Sterling
Photography by the Author

In the center of a desert
highland area in California's
Joshua Tree National Monument stood several palm

Carolina mantis

Lorquin's admiral butterfly

WHY I SHOOT INSECTS

trees, a cottonwood and many small bushes fed by the water of an underground stream. It was a hot September day, and the glaring desert sun filtered down through the green palm leaves. From somewhere, a few hundred feet to my side, came the chi-quer-ke-ker call of a covey of Gambel's quail. In the background, the desert stretched into rocky hills pierced by innumerable sandy gulches. From a makeshift blind, I sat watching the activity of various animals— antelope ground squirrels, doves, warblers, hummingbirds and insects. A waterhole was only 20 feet away.

I observed the toil of the bees constantly descending to the water's edge, landing to drink and flying away again on their journey to the pollen-laden flowers of a nearby tree: bees who travel close to 300,000 miles on wings that beat 11,400 times a minute to gather nectar for a single pound of honey. I watched as hummingbirds hovered over the water, dipping low now and then to imbibe of its coolness. I saw industrious ant lions restore their conical sandpits which had been destroyed by my careless footsteps. I tried to imagine the area as it appeared

to ground squirrels scampering across the sandy gulch scattering quail in every direction as they played their own version of tag. Before me was a miniature, but bustling, world. I slowly began to think back to what had created in me this wonderment for nature.

My fascination with insects was perhaps at its peak at about the age of 10. I remember looking for them everywhere I went. My constant companions were several small plastic bottles stuffed tightly into my pants pockets in which I collected both beautiful and unusual specimens.

Of the many places I visited, one, in particular, stood out. Behind our house, across a boulevard and pushed into the corner of a large field, was a swamp tightly packed with the active world of many insects. In that world of murky water and green cattails I spent hours catching dragonflies, wasps, butterflies and grasshoppers. I sat at the edge of the water and watched diving beetles grab bubbles and swim away with their silver loads of air. I saw dragonflies maneuver through the air, dipping low, soaring high, constantly moving, always looking for food to swoop into their barbed, curved legs. I wandered through cattails twice my height looking for grasshoppers and encountering, once in a while, a large, green praying mantis as it stalked a butterfly on a yellow sunflower. Perhaps I was a curious sight—a little boy wandering up and down the length of the swamp completely fascinated by the new world I had discovered. But at that age it was possible to imagine that I was a part of that new world— a creature with other creatures, living in the dense vegetation of a swampland jungle.

My fascination with insects, particularly, has never worn off. The closer one looks at their world, the more captivating they seem to become. The closer one looks at them, the more colorful and beautiful they appear. Simple animals, yes; but complex, specially adapted for their environment, with camouflaging techniques that outdo even human attempts, with strength that amazes and quickness that startles. That fascination has taken me many miles to many places in search of many new miniature worlds. That fascination, cultivated so long ago, will likely disappear someday. But until it disappears and until the influence of one elementary schoolteacher wears off, I will attempt to capture on film something of the color of insects and try to convey some of the fascination they have for me.

Euchromiid moth

Green stinkbug

Common red dragonfly

the sad decline of the ALLIGATOR

By Robert Gann

The American alligator is in trouble. At one time, perhaps 30 million of the creatures basked in the sun in a broad arch sweeping across the southeastern United States, from southern North Carolina to eastern Texas. One early explorer described alligators on a Florida river as being "in such incredible numbers it would have been easy to have walked acros on their heads, had the animals been harr less."

No longer. Around 1855, alligator sk products became fashionable, and the anima were slaughtered by the hundreds of tho sands. Today, because of man's depredation

e American alligator population is reduced
remnants found mostly in Georgia's Oke-
nokee Swamp, in Louisiana bayous and,
pecially, in the Everglades, the giant swamp
cupying most of southern Florida. And even
ese are going. Last year, poachers—who
egally hunt alligators for their skins—killed
0,000 in Florida alone. "We now count the
ligator as a seriously endangered species,"
ys Herbert M. Mills, executive director of
e World Wildlife Fund.

Somehow it's hard to work up much love
or an animal usually pictured as doing little
ut waiting for someone to fall into the water.
ut the fact is that alligators are not usually
elligerent to man except when molested. The
nimal that does attack humans is his narrow-
nouted cousin, the crocodile. Only a few of
ese have survived in the wild state in the
nited States. There is no proof on record
f an unprovoked gator attacking a man.

Furthermore, the alligator does a lot of
ood in the swamp, so much that some con-

Photo by Leonard Lee Rue III

servationists feel he is essential. During droughts,
as the water level drops, he digs his hole deeper
until it often is the only spot around still holding
water. Bobcats and raccoons use it as a watering
place. Fish swim in it. Birds nest in the still-
green foliage. Turtles, crawfish and frogs are
drawn to its mushy bottom. Without it a lot of
other wildlife would die.

The American alligator, *Alligator mississip-
piensis,* is found only in the U.S., while its only
close relative, *Alligator sinensis,* lives in the
marshes of China's Yangtze Delta. Other cousins are the slender-faced gavials of the Far East,
and the enormous, meek, South American caymen. Those stuffed "alligators," incidentally, sold
in gift shops, are actually imported caymen.

With his awesome jaws, sledgehammer tail
and portable armor, the quick, powerful and am-
phibious alligator looks as if he can take care
of himself. He can, if man would only leave him
alone. After all, he and his relatives have survived for a long time (120 million years, some
scientists claim; certainly since early Bible times,
according to creationist scientists).

To see for myself what is happening to the
gator, I recently spent a few weeks in the Florida
Everglades. I was in the domain of Lt. Tom
Shirley, law enforcement supervisor of the
Florida Game and Fresh Water Fish Commission
—"top cop" of the swamp.

Tom led me through a tour of the glades
one night just as twilight urged the sun below
the far horizon, and a half-moon began to dodge
low clouds. The wind had died. The flat, un-
ending sawgrass, stretching prairie-like to in-
finity, stood smooth and motionless, broken only
by hammocks of scrub willows and redbay.
Through the dusk came the hum of insects, the
rasping purr of a million frogs croaking out of
rhythm, the churrs and chitters of birds ready-
ing themselves for the night and the occasional
splash or yowl or crash of reeds that spotlighted
something large, mysterious, unknown.

We dropped the airboat—an airplane-
propeller-driven skiff hauled behind Tom's car
on a trailer—into a black canal some 20 miles
west of Miami. The air was wet and heavy with
the sensuous smell of breathing vegetation. Tom
banded a spotlight to his forehead, climbed to
an open seat 6 feet above the boat deck and
motioned me to a seat. Then he started the huge

the sad decline of the ALLIGATOR

Photo by N. R. Hallock

prop behind us, and we roared away down a tunnel of blackness.

Expertly, he weaved along the waterway, flashing his light back and forth, swerving, bouncing over solid walls of vegetation, dodging clumps of trees, picking a safe path with uncanny skill. Ahead, snakes swam from our path, turtles ducked in panic, bulgy-eyed bullfrogs floated like pale blobs. An occasional egret, blinded by the light, sprang up in a whirl of wings. Insects streamed toward us; we kept our mouths closed.

At the top of a swaying, 15-foot willow, a raccoon, eyes reflecting the searchlight, peered astonished at our commotion. A little later a doe lifted her head above a clump of rushes, pointed her ears toward us, then whirled and disappeared.

Suddenly Tom raised his arm and pointed. Two hundred feet ahead a ruby-red light glinted in the water. We approached, and it became two tiny lights. Tom cut the motor and we coasted. The lights were the reflecting eyes of a yard-long alligator floating in the water. It slapped its tail and ducked under a grass clump.

A little later Tom spotted another, this one only about 10 inches long. He reached over and scooped him up; and the gator, amazed, opened his mouth and hissed like a turtle. Tom handed him to me, then directed his lamplight into the reptile's mouth to reveal the flap of skin that seals the throat so he can submerge with his mouth open. The animal's eyes, I saw, were equipped with transparent lids to enable him to see under water, and his nostrils were like little snorkels.

The alligator bent double, then straightened,

and the strong little tail slapped my wrist smartly. It stung. An adult alligator can break a man's leg with his tail. "But if you don't bother the gator, he'll not bother you," said Tom. "A gator isn't an aggressive creature, unless you've got one cornered or are messing around a mother's nest."

I returned the baby to the water; and he sank to the bottom, death still. He was slowing down his heart, I knew, preparing for a long submergence. Experiments have shown that adult alligators can hold their breath under water for some 2 hours at a time by slowing their heart beats.

"Now," said Tom, "I want to show you a gator hole. I see one ahead." We cruised to the edge of an island of willows and button bush. Inside was a pond 20 feet across, abandoned now, and filling with aquatic weeds and silt.

An alligator forms his hole, his home, with

Photo by D. W. Pfitzer

Photo by D. W. Pfitzer

care. He scoops out a depression in the mud with his snout, then tears out the vegetation and roots with his teeth and forefeet, slaps the material together and piles it up with his tail. Then he digs a tunnel-like horizontal burrow, a den, in the side. Eventually, trees root in the doughnut-like mound around the pool, holding the soil in place, and eventually a dense hammock or island is formed. Since these ponds are often passed on from generation to generation, some of them may have been active for hundreds of years.

A large hole may have as many as ten gators. But during the spring mating season, a bull may roam several square miles, visiting and mating with various females that live in his claimed turf. In his wanderings he helps keep the smaller channels free of weeds.

While roaming, he produces one of the grandest sounds in nature—a deep, booming bellow, unlike any other sound in the wild. The bellows act both to warn off other bulls and to let the cows know he's on the way.

About 3 weeks after mating, the female be-

gins to build her nest, an involved process which can take as long as a week. She gathers sticks, grass and mud in her toothy mouth and builds a mound the size of a dining room table. Then she squirms around on top, digging with her hind legs until a hollow forms, into which she lays 20 to 60 eggs. She shoves mud and grass over them, smooths the top, then eases herself into the water, exhausted. As the nest material begins to decompose, it heats and acts as an incubator, keeping the eggs at temperatures of 80° to 100° F.

For about 2 months the female guards the nest, wetting it during hot, dry days, repairing the top when rains threaten to wash the mud away, protecting it from raccoons, snakes and human beings.

When the 8-inch young gators hatch, they call with high-pitched oinks for mother. She scrapes and bites away the half foot of sod, freeing them. Then everyone splashes off for a swim and maybe a meal.

A mature alligator will devour nearly anything that moves—garfish, snakes, armadillos, even dogs. But in some areas, according to a recent study by Florida biologists, much of the baby gators' food consists of snails and crawfish.

The female alligator is a good mother—one of the few reptiles to show a tender concern for her offspring. For a couple of years the young hang around home. Then, when they are a yard long and relatively safe from predators, they set off on their own. They'll continue to grow a foot or more a year for the first 6 years, the breeding age, then slow down. Mature females stretch to about 8 feet, males to 10 or more. At one time 15-foot giants were not rare.

As Tom and I were about to leave the gator hole, Tom tipped his head back and sniffed the air. "Smell that? Something's rotting around here." We looked through the brush and found the source: three dead alligators, 3 to 5 feet long, their belly section stripped away. "Poachers," said Tom sadly. "Four, five days ago, I'd say. You see, they take only the belly skin; most of the rest is too tough.

"The problem of the poacher is overwhelming," he continued. "We have fewer than 25 law enforcement officers to cover more than a million acres." In order for an arrest to

the sad decline of the ALLIGATOR

stick, a poacher must be caught with an alligator skin in his possession, an extremely difficult trick, because when he is apprehended in the swamp, he simply throws the rolled-up skin overboard, and it sinks from sight, usually forever.

Today's poachers are tightly organized, too, and have equipment rivaling that of the police: swift airboats, giant halftracks, outboard motorboats, two-way radios to warn of approaching wildlife officers, jeeps and trail motorcycles to ride along the levees and even planes.

They can afford such equipment because there's money in hides. The current market price is $5 to $6.50 a foot, and rising. Men's alligator shoes retail for $70, and a prime alligator suitcase will sell for as much as $1000. The rewards of hunting are high compared with the risk.

One method—more successful than most—is a combination air and land operation. One typical night I rode along with Tom in the spotter plane to see what it was like. Even at 1000 feet, the smell of the glades was in the air, while far on the east horizon the lights of Miami spread like blue-green, phosphorescent mist.

A dozen times in the wilderness below, lights appeared like lost stars. Most were the steady, yellowish lamps of fishermen. Then we caught sight of a flash and a sweep from a beam—on for a few seconds, then off.

"Probably a poacher," said Tom. "That's a working light."

He turned to the radio and called one of the patrol cars below. "Clem, where are you? Okay. Check out a light 3 miles south of the Trail, toward the dike by the pumping station there." Shortly, the officer reported that the poacher—if it had been one—had quit for the night.

Later that evening I transferred from the plane to one of the patrol cars. Tom, still in the plane, spotted another suspicious light in our area. Officer Jim Sistrunk and I were on a dike, a dozen miles from the main road. By moonlight, he had driven with his lights off, and we had been waiting for maybe 2 hours.

Jim accelerated until we were whistling along that narrow levy at perhaps 40 mph, still with no lights, the airboat trailer bouncing behind. At the end of the dike trail we transferred to Jim's airboat, and soon were roaring down the meandering waterways. The sound was deafening, but anyone in another airboat couldn't hear us approach unless he stopped.

Soon we came to a clearing, and across it was another airboat—stopped, and silent. The two rough-hewn men, with a touch of wary defiance, insisted they were frogging. Jim looked the boat over. He found no guns or hides—or frogs.

"I happen to know those guys are poachers," he said later. "But I just can't nail them. Been trying for 2 years now."

A few evenings after my night with the officers, I had an opportunity to hear the poacher's side. Late in the afternoon I received a mysterious call from someone I'll call Big Jack. "I hear through the grapevine you're writing an article on the gator," he said. "Well, I bet you've got most of your stuff from the cops. I was just thinking—maybe I can give you some information of interest—a view, shall we say, from the other side."

Tall, heavy, burned umber by the sun, Big Jack is a day laborer, he told me, with an annual income of $6000. He supplements it with $4000 from the sale of alligator hides. He said he was talking to me because "reporters never got the facts right." Big Jack has been poaching for 7 years. He hunts only during the dry months—March to June—about 4 nights a week. "I'm not considered a big gator hunter. Not until I make at least $10,000 or $12,000 a year from them."

With Big Jack driving my car, we toured some of the more accessible parts of the glades, covering a total of 83 miles. His basic technique, I learned, is to run an airboat along a canal until he spots a pair of alligator eyes, then shoot between them with a .22. "This stuns him," he says. "Then I jab him with a gig, a pipe with two shark-fishing hooks braised to it, and he rolls over and over, wrapping himself in the rope. Then I just haul him in and whack him behind the head with a machete. I can skin em in about 3 minutes—no trouble at all, unless he's come to.

He salts the skins and leaves them in a secret place out in the swamp, rolled up in 5-gallon oil cans. "The most dangerous part is taking the skins out. This way I get them all out together every 3 months, when the dealer comes through. I get outfitted in fishing gear and pretend I'm a

To avoid disturbing the 20 to 60 eggs in the alligator nest, John Holt reached in and pulled out the leathery egg seen in the palm of his hand.   Photo by D. W. Pfitzer

tourist." One poacher, who owns a plane (about a dozen have planes, says Big Jack), takes his skins to the cross-Florida Tamiami Trail, then by radio directs his brother to him. The plane lands on the road right after dawn when there's little traffic, and flies off with the skins. Most hides find their way to processors in the New York or Chicago area who pay about $20 a foot.

"Those canals really make it easy for us," he added. "When the water drops and the gators begin to run out of water, they head for the canals. Once a gator gets there, I figure his life-span to be 24 hours. The only trouble—we got to work awful fast. Because pretty soon there ain't going to be any gators left."

I asked him if he ever worried about getting caught. He laughed. "If I get caught I'll just have to work a little harder to pay off the fine." Penalties go to $1000 and a year in jail. But judges rarely fine more than a couple of hundred dollars, and almost never impose a jail term. Those poachers not let off entirely are usually given insignificant fines, and the softness of penalties is the big complaint of law enforcement men. "We have

good laws in Florida," says Lt. Shirley. "We have adequate fines and sentences—if only the judges will pass them out. But in 1968, here, crime *does* pay." Officer Sistrunk once arrested a man with 42 skins in his boat. He admitted he killed even more, but he left those too large to handle. He was fined $200. The skins were estimated to be worth nearly $1000.

Poachers convicted in Florida between mid-1961 and this January paid an average fine of only $79. Such curious leniency actually *invites* poaching.

Making penalties realistic is one way to help prevent alligators from sliding into oblivion. Perhaps the most important thing to be done—and on this nearly everyone agrees—is to pass national legislation to make it a federal offense to transport illegal skins across state lines. Even Big Jack admits that if poaching were against U.S. law, "I for one would get out of it. Somehow it's different when you're messing with the federal boys. I'd retire."

Such bills are now in the process of being submitted to Congress. One, developed by Sen. George Smathers of Florida, applies strictly to alligators, while the other, the Endangered Species bill, jointly presented by Rep. John D. Dingell of Michigan, and Rep. Alton Lennon of North Carolina, would apply to a number of animals in distress. Both, in the view of conservationists, are excellent.

The most important weapon to level against the poacher, however, is economic; if the profit could be taken out of hunting, it would stop. Around 1900 the beautiful egret was sliding toward extinction because women were paying high prices for plumes. Then, largely because of the efforts of Audubon societies, people became aware that by buying plumes they were helping to kill off the egret. Soon plumes went out of style. Federal legislation was then passed making the possession an offense. The egret was saved.

The same thing could be done for the alligator. Almost all genuine alligator shoes, handbags and suitcases—97 percent of them is one guess—come from illegal sources. As one conservationist put it, "people should be *embarrassed* to wear alligator items—and stores should certainly be ashamed to sell them."

As part of our American heritage, and as a link in the precarious chain of balance in the swamp, the alligator deserves better than to be skinned alive for fashion.

HE SEES

The 300-pound good-natured dolphins appear to have a perpetual smile.

WITH HIS EARS

By Josephine C. Walker

When you hear the word *dolphin,* do you think of an amusing prankster in a pool at a Florida or California beach? a good-natured clown who leaps out of the water on command? or TV's Flipper?

If you do, you're right. The dolphin is all of these things. But you're only half right. The dolphin is more—much, much more—than a tourist attraction or a television star.

He is one of the sonar experts of the animal kingdom, with such unique traits that he has "joined" the Navy to be studied and observed. Eventually he may be used in defense work, possibly even to help spacemen. And all because of one unique trait—he literally "sees" with his ears.

The dolphin has some unusual physical characteristics. In the first place, most people think of him as a fish. This is not so. He's an air-breathing mammal. He usually reaches eight to twelve feet in length. He can stay underwater six minutes without coming up for air. He breathes through a single nostril, a crescent-shaped blowhole on top of his head. This is also the source of his voice, for he can vibrate it like a human lip. He hears through a cushioned inner ear and has one of the keenest auditory senses of any animal. His eyes have lids which look almost human, and they shine like a cat's.

In addition, the dolphin has a perky, saucy personality and what appears to be a perpetual smile. He seems to enjoy living in society. As long ago as A.D. 100 Plutarch said, "To the dolphin alone, beyond all others, nature has granted what the best philosophers seek—

friendship for no advantage. Though it has no need at all of any man, yet it is a genial friend to all and has helped many."

For centuries dolphins amused and delighted fishermen, sailors and ocean travelers as they watched them leap and dive about in the sea. They've been called pranksters of the sea and seagoing cowboys because of their skill at herding fish. Yet, until the early 1900's, no one took them seriously. Scientists ignored them; only a few were aware of the unusual traits and potentials of these 300-pound, good-natured mammals, even though fishermen told frequent stories about their remarkable feats.

The dolphin has a bigger brain than an ape, and many scientists think he is smarter. Some marine biologists believe he may have as high a potential IQ as man—that his brain is so similar to a human brain that he might even be taught to talk. Every animal expert places the dolphin close to the top of the list of animal intelligence.

He swims incredibly fast and has been clocked at 30 miles an hour, overtaking and keeping ahead of some of the fastest liners. He's an expert at herding fish and killing sharks. One fisherman wrote, "Once while fishing I saw a big shark hurl itself from the water, then plop back. Moving closer, I saw that six dolphins had him surrounded. One by one they went in for a torpedolike attack, punching him just behind the gills and in the stomach. The shark finally collapsed and sank to the bottom."

Dolphins have a large number of sounds for an animal without vocal cords. They are the only real mimics among mammals. They make

109

Though air-breathing mammals, baby dolphins are born underwater. They may weigh up to 30 pounds and are approximately 3½ feet long.

Photo courtesy of Marineland of Florida

many sounds—whistling, mewing and rasping—all through the blowhole at the top of the head. One scientist working with dolphins said, "He mimicked my voice so well that my wife began to laugh—and then he gave a fine imitation of her laugh." Whistles seem to be their means of communication with each other. The director of Marineland in Florida once studied the constant whistling between a mother and daughter who had been separated for a time.

Above every other characteristic, though, the most valuable trait of the dolphin is his sonar system. During World War II man perfected a sonar system greatly needed by submarines which made it possible to locate objects by sound waves. The system helped, but it was impossible to tell what object the sound was hitting—a whale, a rock or other object. In studying dolphins, scientists realized they must have a unique sonar system superior to their own. They swim too rapidly in a murky sea for them to rely on sight alone. As captives in a pool, they turn corners skillfully and swiftly. Scientists decided to learn more.

In experiments it was impossible to blindfold a dolphin because it would cover the blowhole on top of his head, smothering him. The experimenters finally used suction cups to cover his eyes to test his ability. To their amazement, he swam sightless just as he had before, unconcerned by his blindness. When a fish was thrown into the water, the dolphin made a grating sound and swam directly to it. Further experiments showed that dolphins were able to differentiate between the food fish of different sizes by hearing the echoes reflected from the fish bodies. In experiments to get at the fish, the dolphin was given a choice of swimming through an open door or crashing through a glass door. In over 200 trials, blindfolded, the dolphin never once attempted to go through the glass door. He can indeed see with his ears.

The Navy has a dolphin school in the Pacific to learn how man may best take advantage of their abilities. Dolphins are trainable, gentle and highly intelligent. It is possible, even probable, that they may become cooperative animals—like St. Bernard dogs for rescue work or seeing-eye dogs for the blind. It may be that through their sonar-locating abilities they can retrieve like dogs, be used in defense work and even help aquanauts.

The dolphin may teach us other things, too. A study of his speed performance may eventually have a dramatic effect on ship design. Even a study of the dolphin's skin has helped scientists. One such man was working on a device for ships to reduce friction drag.

When he crossed the ocean to America, he watched the delightful creatures swimming effortlessly. When they moved through the water, it stayed relatively calm while ordinarily water around any moving object is disturbed. The scientist felt there must be something unusual about dolphins' skin to allow them to control the condition of the water flowing by them. After thorough study, he devised a kind of double coat or hide for use on ships' hulls, making it as nearly like dolphin hide as possible. As a result, the drag was reduced by as much as 60 percent.

Keiki is a very special dolphin working with the Navy in Hawaii. As part of his training, he has been taught to follow a powerboat. Using electronic sound gear, which he is trained to answer, those in the boat forge ahead of him, then turn on the underwater signal. Keiki surges forward, sometimes leaping from wave to wave until he overtakes the boat. He has picked up the signal from as far as 350 yards. Throughout each test, Keiki performs as though he is playing games with his human friends—which indeed he is.

In scientific experiments, the animal's intelligence is often like that of a human being. When one scientist touched a pleasure area in a dolphin's brain with his electric brain-stimulating machinery, the dolphin liked the sensation so much that he learned to hit the switch for more. When the doctor rearranged the switch so that this was no longer possible, the dolphin literally blew his top, making angry noises through his blowhole. When the doctor hit an area in the dolphin's brain associated with unpleasantness, the dolphin learned to turn off the current.

This highly intelligent 300-pound playboy amuses thousands and, at the same time, aids the Navy in its research.

Dolphins are easily trained to perform tricks
but also appear to enjoy playing
with balls and other objects on their own.

Animals

By Bonnie-Jean McNiel

Photography by Oran McNiel

*They look like flowers,
eat like animals and
live in the ocean depths.*

Having received my initiation to the wonders within the sea in warm and temperate waters, the question propelling itself around in my head as we moved to the Pacific coast was, "How can those cold waters sustain any sort of life compared to the glorious, vivid colors and life of the warm seas?" It was with some negative feelings and prejudiced ideas that I suited up, turned on my air and somersaulted into the kelp-filled, sheltered cove.

Suspended, weightless, in 70 feet of hazy liquid filled with gently swaying kelp, I felt the first searching fingers of icy, 46-degree rivulets discovering passageways into my scuba suit. "Whatever scenery is down here," I said to myself, "had better be worth this torment."

Briskly descending the anchor rope through the strands of kelp, I came to the wall of rock I was seeking; there the door to the world of the "flower animals" (Anthozoans) opened before me. The first of my doubts began to dissolve as I gazed in awe at the beauty I had never dreamed possible.

Extending its feathery, branching tentacles above its thick muscular body was a plumose anemone (Metridium). Its delicate, lacy fringe of tentacles moved rhythmically with the surge, capturing only the microscopic animals called

LEFT: The mushroom-shaped plumose anemone waves its lacy fringe of tentacles rhythmically with the current of the ocean floor. The creature feeds upon microscopic plankton.

TOP: Because of its ability to fluoresce, the coral-colored gregarious anemone can be seen at great depth. This anemone was photographed 80 feet underwater.

BOTTOM: The sticky nodules encircle the green anemone attracting prey to adhere to its surface.

113

Flower Animals

plankton. This brought to mind the fact that the clarity of the cold Pacific coast waters is often directly proportional to the amount of plankton growing. Peering into the forest of those waving fingers ringing the edge of the anemone's rayed disk atop its stout body, I saw its stretched-out mouth with its finely sculptured grooves funneling water and food into its stomach cavity. It was not my privilege, though, to verify on this dive the fact that these creatures sometimes turn their stomachs inside out in their feeding pattern. Curious to know how it would react to my touch, I placed both hands about its muscular stalk and applied gentle pressure. Within six seconds that magnificent, fragile-looking animal folded into itself; and, instead of being a stately ten inches tall, it became a wrinkled, flat two-inch leathery pancake.

The face of the rock beside the plumose anemone was covered with the dainty little disks and bodies of the vivid coral-colored gregarious anemone (*corynactis californica*). Since reds filter out first, it puzzled my buddy and me that the red was so distinct at an eighty-foot depth until we realized it was because this particular anemone fluoresces. It was easy to see that in colonies like this only the ones on the outer fringes could take part in the asexual reproductive budding process. The individuals in the center would just not have any place to spread if they decided to divide themselves after their kind.

Floating down toward a crevice between two vertical cliffs, I spied two large green anemones (*Anthopleura xanthogrammica*) with

The dahlia anemone is equipped with stinging cells which paralyze large prey, such as crabs and small fish, satisfying its carnivorous appetite.

their fifteen-inch centers enticing all curious prey to land on that circular aerodrome.

Seeing these three caused me to reflect that the things which at low tide looked like little bowls of jello with bits of sand and shell stuck in at odd angles were really these anemones using some of their sticky nodules about their column to adhere various items for camouflage. Within the tissue of these anemones and their close relatives, the aggregated anemones (*Anthopleura elegantissima*), there live plantlike cells. Therefore, in bright sunlight the plantlike cells give the aggregate anemones their bright emerald green color. Sometimes they dress themselves with streaks of pink or lavender. Speaking of coloration, some anemones relate to their food supply, and they come in many colors, hues and variations—white, salmon pink, tan, orange, brown, green, red, striped and dotted, and not infrequently mixed.

Any lingering doubts I may have had concerning the lack of color in these waters went rushing with my bubbles to the surface when I came upon the open center of the aptly named dahlia anemone (*Tealia felina*) with its complementary ring of fat-based, tapering tentacles, each crowned with its own bud of stinging cells. Closed, it resembled a luscious ripe tomato with white spots. Later I learned that the dahlia anemone is carnivorous and feeds on relatively large prey, such as crabs and small fish, capturing them with its dexterous tentacles, paralyzing them and then folding them into its mouth. Upon further observation, I discovered that some anemones have a literal hangover after a heavy meal—their usually active tentacles all droop over into a stringy mass. In a few days they revive.

On the rolling bottom in a relatively protected "private lot" rose the semihardened encasement of the tube anemone (*Cerianthus aestuari*). It was buried completely except for two inches below its feeding disk, from which delicate tentacles whipped out in a radius of five inches. It seemed more sensitive than the other kinds of anemones I had so far encountered, for just the shadow of my hand caused it to retract down its protecting tube in a flash. This behavior was easily explained when I learned that it builds this protective tube because it cannot fold into its column like the plumose or aggregate anemones.

Moving back to the rocky ground, I took a stalk of *Macrocystis* kelp in my hand and searched along its stem and broad-leaved fronds, hunting for the little red anemone (*Epiactis prolifera*) reported to be common from the Puget Sound south. It is a small (¾ of an inch across) anemone with the curious life pattern of sheltering its young inside its body cavity and then transferring the juveniles to brood pouches around the outside of its column. Finding one of these would be an exceptional experience, I felt; but, alas, the search was fruitless.

I knew there were different ways for an anemone to reproduce, one being similar to the starfish: If a chunk tears off, that piece reproduces, as well as the original mending. The process which fascinated me most was the complete body rupture of one anemone (*Diadumene luciae*), which is common to both the east and west coasts, resulting in the formation of any number of various parts of the body. All in all, this system of reproduction develops some pretty messy scenes.

Pondering all the wonders of this world of the flower animals, I surfaced to the warmth of the bright sunlight, my mind's eye still dazzled by the spectacular beauty within this fascinating world of cold water. Subsequent reading has taught me that, contrary to what I had first thought, sea anemones move around at times by themselves and also by some friendly persuasion. For instance, a smart hermit crab within his acquired shell home will sidle up to an anemone and rub steadily and gently against its base. In time the anemone will transfer onto the shell house of the crab, and the hermit crab has his built-in paralyzing unit. These two then enjoy communal living —the crab receiving protection from the sting of the anemone and the anemone eating scraps left over from the crab's unrefined and sloppy feeding habits. There are also some crabs in warm waters that go around menacingly waving an anemone in each claw, presumably for protection.

The reverse of this communal living project of the hermit crab and anemone is apparent between the some one dozen species of anemone fishes (*Amphiprion*) and their anemone hosts. The gaily decorated clown fish (*Amphiprion percula*) swim in and out through the anemone's deadly tentacles without any ill effects. Its immunity to the paralyzing venom of its host comes from its capability to secrete a mucus which prevents the anemone from exploding its stinging cells. The clown and the anemone get along well together. The fish attracts other small unimmunized fish to the anemone's eager clutches, and the clown feeds on leftovers regurgitated by the anemone and hides from predators with a taste for clown fish.

Anemones are only one of the fascinations of the underwater world waiting for those who dare to penetrate its depths.

Flower Animals

Florida's last frontier

By Norman R. Hallock

With the passing of time, man is gradually crowding himself on every side. Realty firms are constantly buying up farms and, ere long, drained fields take the place of depressions from which amphibian choruses have serenaded the countryside for generations.

We can be thankful for some farseeing individuals who have helped to set aside unspoiled areas for our enjoyment and the enjoyment of future generations. Certain areas of our nation require a great deal of studied attention to give balance to farming and habitation and, at the same time, allow wildlife to remain undisturbed.

A good example of such studied attention is the effort being waged in southern Florida to keep vital forces in balance. Although the Everglades National Park—our third largest—was established in 1947, the nearly 1½ million-acre tract could become a desolate, desiccated area within a short time.

The Florida Everglades are unique in their saucer-like flatness. This vast area cannot boast of an elevation greater than about 10 feet above sea level. One is reminded of this as he drives perhaps halfway across southern Florida and then comes upon a neat road sign reading, "Rock Reef Pass, Elevation Three Feet." So nearly level is this Floridian plateau that there is less than a 2-inch drop in elevation per mile for many miles.

A glance at a map showing Florida's topography reveals the large inland Lake Okeechobee whose southern shore is about 125 miles from the tip of the state. For centuries, waters from much of central Florida drained into this body of water, largely through the Kissimmee River. These in turn flowed out of their southern shores and began the long, slow journey of less than a half mile per day over the almost flat country to the south.

Along the southeastern coast of Florida is an outcropping of limestone known as Miami oolite. Its elevation is but a few feet, and along the western coast there is, likewise, a slight rise in the terrain. Between is a slightly tilted area more than 50 miles in width and nearly twice as long. For many centuries minor seasonal changes, such as fluctuations in rainfall, produced no major changes.

Then, in 1928 a hurricane tore into Lake Okeechobee and blew much of its water out onto the populated communities. Some 2,000 persons perished, and the disaster resulted in more attention from the Federal Government. The now-almost-completed Herbert Hoover Dike, along with numerous costly canals and embankments developed through the years, now controls billions of gallons of water. Water can be pumped either into or out of the lake. Vast reservoirs to the south of the lake help to impound the waters;

Purple gallinule

Florida's last frontier

and, by careful control, a recreation area and permanent natural habitats for many forms of wildlife are maintained. The level of the lake is lowered before each hurricane season in order that the 1928 tragedy may never recur.

The Tamiami Trail now makes use of one of the east-west embankments. A straight-as-an-arrow, 90-mile stretch of fine road saddles the south bank of the big ditch. Its six sets of gates can be seen from the road. Perhaps the naturalist-minded person may be interested in the fauna and flora of the region. It should be pointed out that little of either would be left were not wisely planned and executed engineering projects provided.

As the traveler enters the Everglades National Park from the east, he soon comes to a set of modern buildings that serve as headquarters for a staff of well-trained park personnel. Courteous answers are given to the many questions asked daily by many visitors.

Several days, weeks or even months can be spent profitably here in Florida's last frontier. At least two safe, sufficiently lighted areas are available to campers. Each is supplied with sev-

Photo by W. Daniel Sudia

eral clean restrooms. The many tree frogs appreciate these as much as do the people—but for different reasons. The little green blobs are eager consumers of insects attracted to the lights; and 50 or more may be seen on the walls, windows and ceilings most any night.

The fine road through the park is well marked. There are several important points of interest. The first stop will leave a lasting impression. The map tells the traveler that he has reached Royal Palm where are found the famous Anhinga and Gumbo-limbo Trails. Here he will want to spend considerable time. It is best first to take the guided tour, and then return over the same walk

—perhaps many times—for different types of wildlife will be seen each time.

Upon looking over the stone wall, which keeps one from falling into the adjacent pond, a visitor may be startled to gaze into the eyes of a 12-foot alligator quietly enjoying Florida's 80° sunshine. The gator may be not more than 2 feet away, and the wall feels exceedingly welcome. Should this be a female, she may be accompanied by the remains of her last hatch of young alligators, the rest having been devoured by a hungry father or, possibly, by large snapping turtles.

Looking out over the placid pond, one may see what he thought to be a dead log suddenly open its mouth or slowly sink to the bottom— just another gator!

What a place! Things are happening all about —usually in the direction of the pond. Someone is heard to exclaim, "Oh, look at that snake swimming with its head held out of the water." One better versed in Everglades life quietly informs him that the creature is the anhinga or water turkey, sometimes called the "snakebird."

Just to the right of where he may have been observing the anhinga for the past half hour, the visitor will notice other birds. The largest one will probably be seen first. This bluish-gray monster at the edge of the bank stands about 4 feet high. It is the great blue heron. He cautiously watches a fish, frog or crustacean that has ventured too near for its own safety. Suddenly the neck arches downward, and the long pointed bill is thrust into the water. There is one less fish or whatever creature it was that drew its interest.

Likely to be seen along the same bank is the American egret, almost as large as the great blue heron. These great white birds with long, shiny, black legs are also superb fishers.

About 300 species of birds are found in the Everglades, and a trip around the Anhinga Trail will add a sizable number to a birdwatcher's list. One never to be forgotten is the purple gallinule whose long, yellow toes distribute its weight so that it nimbly walks about on the spatterdock leaves, constantly searching for food. This bird is not a swimmer.

To the right, one may hear calls for friends or relatives to come and look into the water as huge numbers of garfish (12 to 15 inches in length) almost cut off the view of green water vegetation below. The slight motion of their fins keeps them stationary as the water rushes past them and over the low falls under the bridge. Great numbers of smaller fish are also in evidence. Garfish are the main "bill-of-fare" for alligators, according to William B. Robertson, Jr., park biologist.

Photo by Norman R. Hallock

120

Photo by Norman R. Hallock

Left: Snowy egret

Above: The fruit of the pigeon plum is not too palatable, but will sustain life.

Florida's last frontier

Interspersed among the saw grass are found many colorful flowers, such as the scarlet swamp milkweed and crimson morning glory. Other areas have an abundance of yellow spatterdock and blue pickerelweed. A rather attractive shrub, the pigeon plum, produces colorful fruit which, though not too flavorful, is said to have sustained human life when other foods were not available.

Due to the preponderance of water during much of the year and also the continued shade of hammock areas, one finds an abundance of epiphytic plants, most of which are not parasitic. These include many species of colorful orchids. Members of the pineapple family, known as bromeliads, grow to large dimensions in their arboreal positions. Extending from many tree trunks is the resurrection fern. Though they may appear dead or dying, the next rainfall may completely revive these dainty ferns.

The Flamingo area brings one to the end of his land journey. Here in this last frontier portion of Florida one can still find large panther tracks in the muck near his pathway. Now and then these graceful cats are seen in daylight hours. Under protection their numbers may be increasing. As Jim Markett and I were traveling along the canal bank, a young bobcat stepped out into the open for a momentary survey of the countryside. Occasionally, black bears are also seen in the Florida Everglades. Deer are quite plentiful, as well as raccoons, otters, minks and squirrels. These all are similar to northern animals and are not considered tropical.

The coastal waters contain many playful and intelligent porpoises, as well as sharks. Manatees, or sea cows, whose food consists of the abundant green vegetation, are found in the quiet bays. They thrive well on the channel-choking water hyacinth. Man has encouraged their pasturing in such areas, even to the extent of transporting them to places where these hyacinths grow too profusely. Crocodiles are sometimes found in the warm waters along Florida's southwestern Ten Thousand Islands and in some inland waterways.

Three-hundred-pound loggerhead turtles lumber up the sandy beaches under cover of darkness to deposit their clutches of eggs, their young emerging in about 2 months unless found by some hungry raccoon or other predator.

For the lover of natural beauty, the sunset boat cruise from Flamingo's docks into the Florida Bay is an experience never to be forgotten. The last rays of the sinking sun reveal

121

Florida gallinule and coots

Photo by Norman R. Hallock

Florida's last frontier

thousands of birds winging their way from the mainland and freshwater feeding areas to the numerous secluded, wooded islands offshore. Here predatory animals are limited or completely lacking. In this semitropical environment, the winged creatures come to rest in the dense thickets whose branches bend down with the many species of long-legged, yet graceful, fowl.

During the following morning hours, one may stand along the shores of Whitefish Bay and watch the large flocks of egrets, white ibis and other birds returning to the mainland's waterways. Breathtaking views of the pink roseate spoonbills' graceful flight as they pass directly overhead convince any bird lover that this has been worth the entire cost of a trip to the Florida Everglades.

Besides being the home of countless feathered friends, the Everglades have witnessed untold generations of Indians as they battled with natural forces for an existence. The story of their dealings with the white man, especially the Spaniards, leaves one with a feeling of sympathy for those brave nomads of the forest. Some of their descendants are the Seminole Indians still living along the Tamiami Trail. Their abodes vary considerably. The former type of home—the chickee —a palm-thatched roof supported by four corner poles, is still used by many. This shelter, often without permanent walls and partitions, reveals a simple way of life, yet one strongly affected by modern inventions.

Besides ancient handmade articles, one may find a modern sewing machine being used to produce colorful Indian garb. The operator of this timesaver may be enjoying the outside world as she turns her head to a TV screen resting on a bunk bed nearby. Her children or grandchildren have the privilege of attending a modern school a short distance down the road. As one observes the operation of one of the airboats at speeds up to 60 miles an hour, or even a bit faster, he becomes conscious of the fact that the Seminole can be a good mechanic, and that he adjusts well to the use of modern machines. These Seminoles are also a self-governing tribe.

It takes a trip to the Everglades for one to fully appreciate this unique land of contrasts. Especially to the northerner is it difficult to imagine the sudden change of temperature, the abundance of bird life, some of which seems to have lost the fear of *Homo sapiens,* and the close balance between disaster and luxuriant plant life. Crowded into the southern end of Florida are new challenges to the lover of the outdoors and to the person interested in the secrets of unusual flora and fauna.

Great blue heron

Photo by W. Daniel Sudia

From the canyon below, the author views the twin bridges, their arching undersides and the sheer vertical drop that blocks access to them. Sunlight can be seen between the bridges, on the upstream bridge, clearly showing their twin, parallel nature.

Utah's Gemini Twins

Two elusive sandstone arches discovered, lost, found again

By F. A. Barnes
Photography by the Author

Lin Ottinger is a backcountry guide who operates out of remote Moab, Utah. More than a decade ago, Lin discovered a rare and magnificent phenomenon, a matched pair of natural stone bridges.

The story of Lin's discovery is not a simple one of find-and-report. Rather, it is one of long years of frustration and bafflement, because the Gemini Bridges, as we came to call them, were exceptionally well hidden within a gigantic system of wild and mazelike canyons. Stumbling upon them once, or even twice, did not mean that they could easily be found again. Far from it!

Lin first found his twin bridges in 1957 while prospecting for uranium in the rough country northwest of Moab. He kept the discovery quiet for the simple reason that when he tried to return to the bridges, he could not find them. For an experienced backcountry guide this was more than just irritating and something that he did not care to talk about with just anyone.

Over a period of ten long years, Lin made sporadic attempts to relocate his lost twin bridges. He even searched by plane, but the elusive bridges remained hidden.

I met Lin soon after I made my own personal discovery of eastern Utah's wonderland of red-rock canyons. After a few days' acquaintance, he told me, wistfully, of his lost twin bridges. Before I left Moab several weeks later, I told Lin, "You find those bridges again, and I'll help make sure they stay discovered." This must have inspired him, for about a month later I received a letter saying, "I found them!" The following summer I scheduled a trip to see the rediscovered bridges.

We set off enthusiastically in Lin's back-

125

country vehicle, first on pavement, then on a crude dirt trail that often became nothing more than a pair of faint tire tracks through drifted sand or across solid rock. Our trail agonized up treacherous slopes, crossed razor-backed ridges, labored for miles up wild sandy canyons past tall pillars and shapes of looming pink and white sandstone, then finally clawed its way up onto a high, crazily tilted plateau scored and broken by a thousand gullies, rocky draws and crevices. It was a mad tumble of sand and rock, brush and scrub juniper, ravaged by appallingly deep canyons with sheer, vertical walls.

Our laboring vehicle struggled onward for hours. We studied and enjoyed the fantastic scenery that surrounded us, but saw no twin bridges. Lin grew quieter as the hours passed and evening approached. Finally, there was no doubt about it, Lin had once again lost his bridges. What a blow to his pride as a guide!

Thanks in part to a careful study of a topographic map of the area, our next trip met with success. Lin spotted a familiar landmark, pulled our vehicle off the trail a few yards and pointed. "Right there!" he said, with a happy grin.

I jumped out, camera in hand, but saw nothing. Following Lin, I trudged off through the sand and rock for several hundred yards, then stopped abruptly at the edge of an enormous chasm with sheer, vertical walls. And there, just to our right, spanning the upper end of this deep canyon, were Lin's elusive twin bridges!

But what bridges! Lin had said twin bridges, of course, but had not mentioned their size. They were huge! They were colorful! They were gorgeous! They stood side by side, close together yet distinct and separate, each spanning the same deep and unexplored canyon, each soaring in a majestic, colorful arc across a mysterious shadowed gorge of ancient Wingate sandstone.

As I studied them, I realized how they had remained hidden for so long, and why they had been so difficult to relocate. The upper end of the canyon that they bridged made a sharp angled turn so that a person exploring that canyon could not see the angled part from the

The author's wife is shown in the dune buggy the three explorers used to search for the twin bridges.

main canyon, but would have to follow it to its upper end, to the sharp turning, before the bridges would be visible. This had evidently never been done. From above, where we were, the jumbled, tumbled terrain, including the canyon edges and the tops of the bridges, was all roughly the same level, and the canyon was so sharply cut and narrow at its upper end that it was simply not visible until you were virtually at its edge.

But we had found the lost bridges, and they would not escape again, because I had them, and the route to them, carefully plotted on my topographic map. Later, we paced off the distance from the bridges to the nearest quarter-section survey marker, thus getting an accurate measure of their location, and recorded their basic dimensions.

After photographing and measuring the bridges, we set out to get beneath them, because it was soon apparent that only from the canyon below could their true magnificence be photographed. Again, the terrain around the bridges baffled us. There was no way down. The canyon walls were sheer and smooth, and the shortest drop that would give access to the undersides of the bridges was more than 90 feet, with the cliff there deeply undercut. Our only chance to get below was to backtrack for miles, find our way into the vast canyon system below and then into the side canyon that our bridges spanned.

We spent the rest of the day trying this, but by late afternoon found ourselves miles up the wrong canyon. Reluctantly, we gave up our quest for that day, but were determined to return soon.

A few days later we again tried to reach the canyon below the bridges. This time we used a dune buggy, a custom-made, powerful vehicle constructed from a cut-down Volkswagen sedan, so nimble in broken terrain that it made a jeep look like a tortoise.

After hours of beating our way up rocky stream beds, through thick desert brush and over enormous sand dunes, we finally found the canyon we sought. Ours were the first tire tracks ever made in this wild canyon, and we may have also left the first footprints of civilized men.

126

Our twin bridges arched high above us, spanning the secret side canyon that had so long hidden them. Once again our satisfaction was limited. We had hoped to be able to climb up under the bridges from the canyon below, but were prevented by a sheer rock wall more than 100 feet high.

After several hours of admiring and studying and photographing these rare and beautiful natural bridges from the canyon floor, we reluctantly left, but resolved to return with the special equipment needed to penetrate the last of the ancient privacy of these brotherly bridges. We still wanted to stand directly under these majestic stone spans.

It was a full year before we were able to make another attempt. The following September, with the secret of their location still held between us, Lin Ottinger and I returned to the Gemini Bridges. This time we were prepared to get below them from above. We used a large roll of chain ladder and equipment to anchor it to solid rock. After securely fastening one end of the ladder, we carefully lowered it over the cliff.

Lin had the honor of being the first to descend. It was a frightening but thrilling climb down. Once over the lip, the ladder hung free of the cliff, leaving the climber suspended in space almost 100 feet above the jagged rocks below. Still, as Lin descended, his face bore an unmistakable look of triumph. These elusive bridges were truly his at last! When he finally reached the bottom, the canyon walls echoed a victorious shout!

Where are the Gemini Bridges? They are only 17 miles by road from Moab, and can be found with the aid of a 7½-minute topographic map and a little luck, but unless you are an

ABOVE: Lin Ottinger, the bridges' discoverer, drills into solid rock to anchor the chain ladder used to get below the bridges.
BELOW: Lin was the first person down the long chain ladder, once it was lowered over the sheer cliff edge. The climb out was fatiguing, more than 90 feet straight up.

exceptionally good map reader, the only way to see these magnificent and rare twin natural bridges is to visit Moab, contact Lin Ottinger and arrange for him to take you to them. They are presently in no national or state park or monument, although I hope that they will eventually be given such protection. They are close enough to both Canyonlands National Park and Arches National Monument that they could easily be brought under the jurisdiction of either.

Once we had the location of Lin's twin bridges firmly pinned down on a government map, we applied, through official channels, for the right to name them. In due time, we were informed by the U.S. Deparment of the Interior that the Board of Geographic Names had "approved for Federal use the name Gemini Bridges" and that Decision List 6901 would note their exact location and name Lin Ottinger as their discoverer, thus closing the story of the discovery of Utah's Gemini twins.

TABLE	West Bridge (upstream)	East Bridge (downstream)
Length across top	89 feet	70½ feet
Width in center	26 feet	26 feet
Thickness in center	40 feet	18 feet
Depth of canyon below bridge center	100 feet	103 feet
Opening under bridge	60 feet vert. 67 feet hor.	85 feet vert. 44 feet hor.
Maximum distance between bridges 10 feet		

The Gemini Bridges are located about 900 feet along a line drawn 53° east of south from a quarter-section marker located on longitude 109° 42′ 30″, one-fourth mile north of north latitude 38° 35′.

Exploring
Idaho's craters

f the moon / These wilderness lava flows give you the sensation of visiting the astronautical future

By William A. Bake, Jr.

*Photography by the Author,
unless otherwise indicated*

To the apprentice eye the land is chaotic, often to the point of evoking emotion. Barren cratered cones struggle skyward from a bleak, black plain. Deep pits and fissures run jaggedly along and just below the jumbled surface.

This description could be a page from the log of the first lunar landing—but it is not. The place is Idaho's Craters of the Moon National Monument, a land forged by the fires of volcanoes but at the same time garnished by delicate wild flowers, making it an inseparable part of the living earth.

Located in south-central Idaho between Boise and Idaho Falls, Craters of the Moon is part of an extensive area once the scene of volcanic activity. Today it is a place of quiet, darkly beautiful lava flows. The landscape at first glance is one of shocking desolation. From horizon to horizon one sees little but jagged black lava. But closer inspection yields a wealth of natural beauty.

Is it worthwhile for visitors at nearby Yellowstone or Grand Teton National Parks to take the 200-mile trip to the monument? The answer is an unqualified Yes! The impression the monument leaves upon the visitor is a lasting one, imparting a sense of titanic natural forces and man's insignificance. Looking south from atop Inferno Cone at sunset, one is awestruck by the lava wilderness below. No man inhabits the earth as far as the eye can see and beyond. The shadows move slowly, inexorably across the landscape, advancing with the retreating sun, until only a far-away extinct volcano glows in the sunset. Silence presses in. The effect is truly lunar.

So forbidding is this land that settlers long avoided it; and exploration has been relatively recent, mostly in the first quarter of this century. Washington Irving, in his 1868 edition of *The Adventures of Captain Bonneville, U.S.A.*, described the lava flows as "an area of about

LEFT: Spatter cones, such as this one, are formed by aerial bombardments of partially cooled lava. Both the cones and the lava flows appear much as they did when they cooled 2,000 years ago.

Dwarf buckwheat (shown here), bitterroot and monkey flowers spangle Craters of the Moon with carpets of color in early July.

60 miles in diameter, where nothing meets the eye but a desolate and awful waste, where no grass grows nor water runs, and where nothing is to be seen but lava." Indeed, the area is still so undisturbed that scientists often venture into it to seek out islands of vegetation not covered by lava. There they find the original untouched plants of southern Idaho, for neither man nor his animals have ever used these plant islands.

In 1924 the unique character of the lava flows was officially recognized when 53,000 acres were designated as Craters of the Moon National Monument. Today the monument is administered by the National Park Service, which has turned 2,000 acres into a living museum of natural history.

Were it not for the Park Service, the lava would mean little to most of us; but through their efforts today's traveler finds a modern visitor center, a naturalist program, nature walks and interpretive materials. The geology and wildlife of the area are well explained by exhibits at the visitor center. Once familiarized

with the area, visitors usually take a seven-mile scenic loop road through the developed part of the monument.

In early July an amazing array of tiny wild flowers sprinkle the cinder cones along the road with color. Such flowers as dwarf buckwheat, monkey flowers and bitterroot cover the otherwise coal-black material. Since moisture is limited on the porous surface, each tiny plant spaces itself about a foot from the next plant with such perfect precision that some visitors suspect that the flowers were planted, gardenlike, by the Park Service. Later in the summer the plants become dormant, leaving no trace of their jewellike lives.

A great variety of volcanic activity was present in the monument area. Great smooth cinder cones of varying ages dominate some areas, some covered with sparse vegetation, others still barren after more recent eruptions.

LEFT: A wide variety of volcanic activity in Craters of the Moon produced acres of lava, ranging from rough aa lava to the smooth pahoehoe here being studied by a visitor.

TOP RIGHT: A monument naturalist leads a family of visitors through a passageway along the icy floor of Boy Scout Cave. Though the outside temperature may be quite warm, the ice never melts in the monument's various lava caves.

BOTTOM RIGHT: Evening campfire programs are a daily activity at Craters of the Moon's unique campground. A variety of programs acquaint visitors with the geology and wildlife of the monument.

Photography on these two pages courtesy of National Park Service.

In other places, spatter cones built by fire fountains raise their cratered maws skyward. Both types of lava, the smooth cake-batter-like pahoehoe (pronounced pa-hoy-hoy) and rough jagged aa (aa-aa) are found at many points on the nature trails and along the tour road.

Despite the visual impact of the lava flows, visitors often feel that the monument's caves are its most unusual features. Each day during the summer dozens of people can be found exploring the dark recesses of Indian Tunnel, Boy Scout Cave and others. Though the temperatures on the surface can be quite warm, most of these caves contain ice all year. The explanation is that the ice forms during the freezing period of the year (about seven months) and never entirely melts during the summer. Indian Tunnel, the most visited cave, can be reached by a series of steps, and is not entirely dark since occasional shafts of light penetrate from the surface. A lantern is necessary, however, when exploring most of the caves.

This year the monument expects only about 200,000 visitors, a mere drop in the bucket compared to Yellowstone and Grand Teton. One explanation for this light visitation can be laid upon the word *monument*, a word which does not always mean "park" to the general public. Part of the blame can also be put on the climate. Four or five feet of snow is not uncommon during the winter, and summer days are sometimes uncomfortably warm. Plan to arrive at the monument about 3:00 P.M. to avoid the midday heat, and see the sights along the loop road in the early evening and perhaps the next morning.

Overnight accommodations in the monument area are strictly limited to camping. The nearest towns are small and offer few services. Realizing this, the National Park Service has built a modern and highly unusual campground in the lava flows. Each campsite is set down in a hollow with jumbled lava surrounding it, providing each camper with his own "crater." Fifty campsites are available, and the completely modern campground is rarely full. The monument is 20 miles southwest of Arco, Idaho, on good highways.

Those who would explore Idaho's Craters of the Moon will experience a land of subtle and persuasive beauty so unique that memories of it will outlast years of travel. The power of the place is beauty, uniqueness—but more than that, it is perspective.

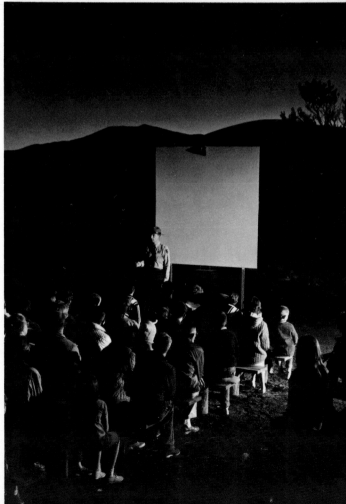

A view toward the Marble Mountains. (Photo by Gilbert Muth.)

Backpacking the Wilderness Trail

By Ervil D. Clark

Continuous rain and cold did not "dampen" the spirits of these college students

Backpacking is not all musing around a campfire as rookie backpackers soon discover. It may be depressingly wet and cold or uncomfortably hot and oppressive, but experience and preparation have a way of making the most adverse situations more tolerable.

A seventy-five to one-hundred-mile pack trip undertaken by my Wilderness Ecology class at Pacific Union College required a great deal of individual as well as group planning. What may appear to have been just a slight lack of care in preparation can sometimes bring near disastrous results.

Joe's feet, for example, were abnormally wide and rather short; he could seldom buy shoes of EEEEEEEE width. Before our hike he found a northern woodsman cobbler who guaranteed a perfect fitting boot that would be both rugged and comfortable. The boots were sturdy enough, but after the first six-mile shake-down hike, Joe had blisters the size of half-dollars. He borrowed a pair of workboots and suffered through the fifty-mile trip, but I doubt if he has hiked since that time.

Rod, on the other hand, had one of the most comfortable pair of boots in the group. For years he had worn them for all types of activities until they fitted his feet perfectly, but he didn't consider the fact that we would be miles from the nearest repair shop when the soles came off and the rotten stitching broke loose. It was a long six miles down to the truck to borrow a pair of my loafers to complete the trip, but it could have been longer. He was fortunate.

Perhaps the most important aspect of preparation centers around the group food supply. High energy, lightweight foods are essential in sufficient quantity and variety to satisfy the appetite and compensate for the extra energy drain during steep, rugged climbs. To achieve this goal nearly all food chosen for the trip is dried, or at least partially dried; and this makes it possible to keep the weight down to about a pound and a half of food per person for each day on the trail. One of the most difficult things to judge is the amount of food a group will consume. When we organized a group of ten which included four girls, we felt that the amount of food could be less than for a group of ten fellows. After we were on the trail, it became apparent that the girls ate as much or more than the fellows, and there was no opportunity to increase the amounts.

Often, as in this case, differences in appetites are not evident until it is too late to make additions to the supply. Jim, for example, waited until we were two days from civilization to tell us that he was used to eating seven sandwiches at noon. It was obvious that we had not planned for such a voracious appetite, and Jim had to make a few changes in his usual routine.

Approximately half of the food was purchased from companies such as Dri-lite and Bernard that package dried foods for backpackers — such as entrees, vegetables, egg products and milkshakes. From a local store powdered milk, puddings, soups, crackers, dried toast, flaked potatoes, macaroni products and other desired items can be added. To keep the weight down, all items purchased locally should be repackaged in double plastic bags with the directions written with a grease pencil on the inner bag. An added advantage is that all packaging materials can be burned in a campfire, leaving no refuse to be carried out or dropped by a careless camper.

The excitement of planning and preparing for such a trip reaches a peak when the day for departure arrives. The first packtrip into the Marble Mountains of northern California, with a group of nineteen students, was a memorable trip of unknowns and unforeseen circumstances. There was a dense fog the morning we left the college and later a steady rain as we traveled northward on the Redwood highway. Rain is unusual for California in early August; but when we arrived at the Ranger Station in Happy Camp, Siskiyou County, we were alarmed to find that the weather forecast called for rain for the next two days. Many hardy hikers laugh at rain and thoroughly enjoy it, but I was more than apprehensive about taking a group of inexperienced and somewhat ill-prepared college students into the cold and misery of rain, sleet and hail at six-thousand-foot elevation.

We arrived at Sulphur Springs campground at the edge of the wilderness area just as darkness was coming on, only to find that a ranger was waiting with a high-powered rifle

Resting on the trail from Bear Lake to Sky High Lake. (Photo by Ervil Clark.)

Cross-country hiking above Red Rock Canyon. (Photo by Ervil Clark.)

for a bear that had been raising havoc around the countryside and in the camps. At his suggestion, we found another location to set up camp and attempted to prepare a hot meal in spite of a steady rain. Here was where some of the preparation paid off. A plastic tarp draped over our shoulders shed the water that would have soaked us to the skin. Waterproof boots helped to keep the feet warm and dry. Some students had not thought it necessary to plan for such an event, and those wearing tennis shoes were soon wet.

While the food preparation crew was struggling with its task, the rest of the group searched for spots to set up their tarps and sleeping bags. For each group of two, a nine-by-twelve plastic tarp went under the two-inch foam pads and sleeping bags while a second tarp served as a tent to ward off the rain. Some made the mistake of placing the tarp in direct contact with the bags, and moisture condensation was nearly as heavy as the rain would have been. A few decided to sleep in the cars for the night, while one group of three laid their bags in an open-bed trailer with a canvas tarp pulled taut over the edges. As the rain continued, the tarp gradually sagged from the weight of water. At three o'clock in the morning, the trio attempted to empty the pool of water from the tarp only to have it spill over the edge and douse them with cold water. Their yells woke up half the camp, and the first thought was that a bear was running off with one of the boys.

After a somewhat interrupted night, we crawled out of our bags in spite of the continuing rain and dreary prospects for the day. We had seven miles to hike and four thousand feet to climb. After a rain-splattered breakfast, we packed our gear, pulled a plastic tarp over our packs and started up Bear Creek trail. It was a relief to be on the trail, and the exercise broke the monotony of rain and cold.

At six thousand feet, with everything thoroughly wet from two days of rain, we became aware of the importance of carrying a few emergency fire-building materials even if it meant a little extra weight. No one in the group had windproof matches, a candle or even a small bit of dry tinder. Cold and miserable, we huddled in small groups cutting shavings and chips from the driest branches that could be found. Some even used precious quantities of toilet tissue, but even this took hold very slowly in the moisture-laden wind. After an agonizing half-hour, fires began to glow and then blaze as more wood was added until flames were leaping fifteen feet in the air. At least the biting cold was being driven back even though the moisture was still present.

As the steaming warmth spread through the group, individuals began to leave the comfort of the fire to clear a place for their tarps and sleeping bags. It wasn't long after the hot supper and a bit of "toasting" at the warm fires that everyone was in bed, exhausted from the strenuous first day of hiking. It was beginning to look more like a wilderness survival course than a wilderness ecology trip.

During the night, with the storm raging over the peaks above and gusty winds plucking at our grove of trees, I learned an important lesson of wilderness survival. There was a loud cracking sound followed by a heavy thud as the broken top of a tree came crashing down. I quickly whipped out my flashlight and

Setting up camp for the night and preparing that good campfire supper. (Photo by Gilbert Muth.)

crawled out of my sleeping bag, fully expecting to find the battered bodies of some of my students beneath the fallen tree. Much to my relief the snag had fallen some fifty feet from the nearest sleeper, but sleep came fitfully the rest of the night as I thought about the importance of checking the tree tops before setting up a camp.

When the gray dawn appeared, students stirred from their bags and slipped on clothing still drenched from the previous day's rain. Two pairs of socks, hanging on sticks by the fire were a jumbled mass of cotton and holes. Heat from the fire had been too much for the nylon threads which had melted and left behind the shapeless cotton cloth. There would be one less change of socks for two fellows in the group.

Thursday night at Lower Sky High Lake saw an end to the storm, but the anticipation of spending another night beneath a damp, whipping plastic tarp drove eight fellows to crowd into a log lean-to cabin built many years ago by cattlemen. Friday morning dawned bright and clear. A heavy mist hung over the lake and in the canyon. The grass in the meadow sparkled with frozen dew. We had weathered the storm and learned some never-to-be-forgotten lessons of the effects of climate upon the environment, but we were two days behind schedule in our purpose of becoming acquainted with plants and animals and the ecology of the wilderness area.

The hills and the valleys, the trees and the flowers had been washed clean; the effect was startling. Birds flitted about in search of food, deer grazed at the edge of the meadow and the spirits of the backpackers took a leap upward. In the distance the gleaming white surface of the marble rim appeared like snow-covered peaks, framed by the green firs and hemlocks.

For the next few days the mountains yielded their secrets to the eager group of students. Beautiful tiger lilies, orchids and monkey-flowers graced the stream bank. On the steep slopes and ridges endemics such as weeping spruce, foxtail pine and Sadler's oak were observed. Methods of conservation were discussed where evidence was found that man had been careless about fire, erosion and littering. Edible plants and fruits were pointed out as emergency food, and open hillsides sprouted with an abundance of squaw root, while many shady, forested areas were covered with blueberry bushes loaded with luscious fruit.

From the top of any high peak in the Marbles, such as King's Castle or Boulder Peak, the view is breathtaking. Mile upon mile of steep ridges and deep canyons clothed with virgin forest stretch out in all directions. To the southeast, Mount Shasta rises majestically above the landscape, while to the south snow-covered ridges of the Trinity Alps glisten in the sun. The depth of its forest green, the brilliance of its flowers, the blueness of its many lakes, the solitude of its eventide — this is what makes the Marble Mountain wilderness the ideal place for study, for recreation and for relaxation.

Although our backpacks are stored away until the snows melt in the mountain meadows, cherished memories of the wilderness constantly come to mind — standing free and alone on a mountain peak, watching the red rays of a sunset color the marble rim, or gazing at the dying embers of a campfire with the moonlight shimmering on the surface of your lake.

SCULPTURE
IN LANDSCAPE

By Mary Vercauteren

Photographs by June B. Aschenbach

A new awareness of art as an expression of nature has been achieved in the making of this outdoor gallery in Vermont

Henry Thoreau wrote, "The lover of art is one, and the lover of nature another, though true art is but the expression of our love of nature."

Along the rest areas of several highways in Vermont, a group of sculptors have challenged both Thoreau's aesthetics and the landscape with large-scale concrete and marble sculptures. The plan, conceived by sculptor Paul Aschenbach of

*A fifteen-ton organic shape of polished black marble by Minoru Niizuma (opposite) rises
seven feet from the ground along Interstate 91 near Hartland. Further north along Interstate 89 near
Waterbury, Dieter Trantenroth has mortared together six large concrete cubes to form a twelve-
foot-high monolith (above) set against the natural splendor of the Green Mountains.*

Charlotte, Vermont, was to demonstrate the feasibility of creating public sculpture at a low cost and which would provide artists an opportunity to work out their own "expressions of nature."

Good fortune and private and governmental approval accompanied the project. The rest areas were public property; the worksite, living quarters for the artists and the artists' time were donated; and much of the raw material was donated or secured by local businesses. Vermont's Governor personally supported the project and the highway commissions were also receptive.

The landscape in which the non-representational pieces were placed by the sculptors is lovely. All too often, however, the highways — those other immense concrete monuments of our civilization — provide a pace that blinds our sight. We fail to see

the wild rose unfurling, the birth of a robin, or the silent tear in a child's eye. Thus, the sculpture was created as much to invite a pause in the pace of American life to provide an opportunity to observe our total surroundings as to point to man's artistic achievements.

Each of the eighteen pieces in Vermont is placed in the midst of a scenic area of striking uniqueness. Some are positioned so they occupy a small portion of a spacious landscape where majestic mountains rise across the distance. There, sweeping, interwoven plains etched with jagged treetops and towering rock buttresses create a complexity of colors, lines and forms. These mountain expanses blend with the foreground, marked by man's attempts on the earth — a red barn, an orchard, a road and a piece of sculpture — each leading the

eye back to a microscopic view of the small growing things at our feet.

The sculpture, set in this vastness, offers a point of anchorage that guides the eye through a momentary flight across the landscape. But when one focuses down on the comparatively small space of the sculpture, the intricate delicacy of nature becomes clear. A tiny yellow buttercup, the sum of innocence and dependence, challenges the sculpture's perfection as its mellow hues reflect on the heavy base of marble or concrete. In its own way, the flower is independent, as if no other ever lived or prescribed a pattern. It projects a totality equal to the mountain or the artistry of the sculpture.

The outdoor gallery, perhaps better than any other art setting, causes one to realize the difficulties of the artist. More than that, it aids us in seeing the immense and fragile, the dumb and vibrant, the fierce and innocent — the diverse and apparently countervailing qualities of nature's universe — in combination and balance. Sculpture in the wild brings one to see and feel a greater harmony than art alone might render. While the sculpture may portray the artist's idea or sensation, nature by contrast exemplifies an interdependence and communion that master artists have been striving toward for centuries.

Groupings of trees or graded valley walls protect some of the pieces in privacy, providing a more intimate contact with nature. Somewhat like a shrine, the cosmic largeness is removed from the setting where nature takes in and houses the sculpture. The trees and shrubs offer comfort and compatibility with the sculptural form.

The sculptures with finer lines and more musical forms, placed on a grassy knoll, arouse a sensation of delight and airiness. Placed in this elevated setting and designed with a buoyant quality, they add to the startling immediacy. The whole landscape is only a touch away — the sound of a brook, the smell of the earth's many fragrances and the blue mist of the sky. The grassy, wildflowered pedestal of the sculpture becomes the elevator to an experience that goes beyond the ordinary.

For each sculptural placement, nature seems to offer the hint of acceptance while the sculpture offers a "cultural stress." The sculpture acts as a sign post or a direction, pointing to the setting rather than demanding all one's attention.

The outdoor galleries are not the kind to whisper and tip-toe in, but a place to enjoy, to see, to touch, climb, to ponder, and most of all, a place to remember. And these galleries are not for an elite. Children adapt more readily to the idea that sculpture, regardless of what it is supposed to be, accommodates their own imaginations. While adults may ponder or admire the tactile forms or surfaces, children discover Trojan horses, secret hide-outs, or mysterious fabrications of giants. The sculpture may become a space mobile for some, while others ride their construction down to the depths of the sea.

As the days and season progress, the sculpture continually becomes a new experience, beyond the varied inspiration it provides each person. The morning crispness is more emphatic. Each dawn illumines a landscape removed from past recollections by the modulations of the sculpture.

The evening holds more evocations as the orange glow of the sky reflects from or infuses the particles of marble and concrete. The orange changes to a blue-crimson as the sun slips further beyond the horizon, and we feel we have discovered a new timepiece. A clock of color, moving from orange to blue-crimson and a deep blue-black, kindled finally by the moon.

With the brightness of day, curious sunlit patches burst forth in a profusion of tones, while the shaded zones lie in a deeper recluse waiting for the light. The sculptural piece, casting shadows and catching the light from the changing positions of the sun, has a sundial effect on the grass and plants around it.

With the changing of seasons, the sculpture is shrouded in foliage, wildflowers, green rolling hills and a mantle of songs from birds and brooks. In autumn, it is encircled in windswept, multicolored leaves and curiously shaped seed pods. The sculpture then takes on an air of the same sense of loss as the trees and hillsides.

In winter the sculpture becomes the resting place for snowflakes, and on the edges ice crystals form. Perhaps a small furry creature will find just the right curve or space in the sculpture to keep him from the blustering cold. In spring the sounds and increased activity prepare the setting for which the sculpture was designed. There is a release toward fulfillment for both art and nature.

Over nine feet high, a white marble sculpture in two pieces by Yanez Lenassi
seems to dwarf nature's immensity along Interstate 91 near Putney.

LEBANON—

The Blessed Land

By G. Gene Johnson
Photographs by the Author

High in the Lebanon mountains the Abraham River roars from a dark cave at the base of a towering cliff, crashes down a steep, rocky slope, and sends up a mystic spray to enshroud the ruins of an old Roman temple. The Romans crossed the mountains each year to perform sacred rituals at this awesome place, and portions of the old Roman road remain today as historic landmarks cut into solid bedrock.

As I walked that ancient road one day, I felt as a trespasser, a man displaced in time, walking back into history, experiencing a brief moment with an earlier civilization. History has indeed left many visible landmarks in Lebanon. Inscriptions, carved

by King Nebuchadnezzar, Napoleon and other conquerors of the past, remain today as antique decorations on canyon walls. The remains of old temples, castles and cities are scattered throughout the country.

Baalbek, in the Bekaa valley, provides the best known and most extensive ruins; Tyre, Sidon, and Byblos are also common tourist stops. And for those who like hiking with their history, and have more than a few days to see Lebanon, there are many other ruins in more remote places.

But the history of the past is no more interesting than the natural history of the present. When naturalists go half way around the world, they of

Opposite: *People of the sea, two Lebanese fishermen stand against the golden-hued Mediterranean.*
Above: *The salt from evaporated sea water is harvested from retaining pools on salt farms.*

course find differences, all begging observation and explanation. At the same time, however, they are struck by familiarity, for the earth's complex web of life has many common threads and nature is never totally different from one place to another.

Land of abundance

From a narrow coastal plain accented by the blue-green brilliance of the Mediterranean Sea, the mountains rise steeply to an average elevation of six thousand feet; then, on the eastern flanks, the mountains drop three thousand feet to merge with the magnificent farmland of the Bekaa valley. Lebanon is thus divided into three contrasting topographical regions, each with its own climate, produce and natural history.

The semitropical coastal plain yields an abundance of citrus fruits, bananas, loquats, grapes and pomegranates, plus a great variety of garden vegetables. From the heavily terraced mountains come tons of apples, peaches, apricots, plums, cherries and grapes, while in the fertile Bekaa valley thousands of acres of agricultural crops form quilted patterns that change with the seasons from the pastel greens of spring to the golden browns of summer. Lebanon is truly a land "flowing with milk and honey," but only because the land first flows with water, that elixir of life, without which all else fails.

Magic mountains

The Lebanon mountains bubble and sing with water. Neither Syria to the north and east nor Israel to the south is blessed with such abundance. The geologic explanation is a layer of non-porous rock lying within the upfold forming the mountains. Because of this layer water is forced to the surface, producing unnumbered springs, some of which have a flow of several thousand cubic feet per second and emerge as small rivers.

An annual rainfall of fifty inches adds further blessings to the earth, setting the stage for a springtime spectacle of wildflowers. Daisies and poppies dance on the hillsides in a wild harmony of color, while hosts of dainty orchids raise their heads in shady places. French lavender, yellow broom, blue lupine and all their colorful cousins join the celebration, making it an event sufficient to bring shame upon all who do not turn their faces toward the earth at such a time.

Against the distant mountains, birds flutter around the ruins of Anjar, its ancient Roman arches sheltered in the fertile Bekaa valley.

As I walked that ancient road, I felt as a
man displaced in time, walking back into history

Top: *Lebanese peasants feel close to their domesticated animals.* Above: *A colorful orange juice shop on wheels rumbles through the city streets.*

Paradise for lizards

The rains come as torrential downpours, mostly during December, January and February. Sunshine and warmth prevail the rest of the year, providing a paradise for lizards.

Every rock is "owned" by a lizard, or so it seems on a warm summer day. And each new spring countless hosts of tiny, transparent baby lizards scramble from leathery eggs hidden away in secret places and scurry-waddle out to find a rock of their own. The competition is great. Even now as I write in my study, a scaly green head with beady eyes moves up and down on the window sill.

Legless lizards, known as glass snakes, are common and sometimes reach a length of three or four feet. Chameleons, the funniest and most fun of all lizards, are also abundant. They have prominently bowed legs, split feet, prehensile tails, hump-backed bodies and eyes imbedded in rotating turrets with independent action. There is simply nothing to compare with the stark, cold stare that comes from one eye of a chameleon, while with the other eye he scans the environment. Chameleons frequently shed their skin and there is perhaps no sorrier sight than a half-grown chameleon midway through a molt. At such times little shreds and patches of old skin hang loosely from all parts of the exotic anatomy.

Predatory insects prevalent

Because there is no real winter in the lower elevations the mysterious cycles of insect life are manifest the year around. This assures the lizards of plenty to eat and assures biologists of having interesting field trips.

Several species of praying mantis make every shrub and bush a trysting place. One species, a stubby, flightless mantis, is surprisingly abundant at high elevations where it blends with the rocks and dwarfed vegetation. Dragonflies, some in striking colors, patrol the water places, while a bewildering array of hunting wasps search for their various prey.

Busy beaches

The Mediterranean Sea is Lebanon's great front yard, a place for work and play with crowded beaches and busy shipping lanes.

Fishing is vigorously pursued for both sport and livelihood. At night the coastal waters are illuminated by hundreds of gas lanterns carried in small fishing boats. During the day many beaches are decorated with a colorful array of fish nets laid out to mend and dry.

On the northern coast the salt water is pumped by windmills into shallow cement retaining pools. On hot days the water rapidly evaporates, leaving a residue of salt which is harvested in burlap sacks and taken to a nearby processing plant.

Contrasts in the countryside

Lebanon not only offers great diversity in topography and scenery but also extreme contrasts

Lifeblood of the land, water feeds the peaceful Lebanese mountains, making their many terraces lush with fruit trees and other vegetation.

in the people and in the technology. While oxen, adorned with blue beads, challenge the rocky soil with a wooden plow in one field, a new tractor, also adorned with blue beads, works in an adjacent field, and on the same road a man on a donkey bumps proudly along, just beyond the reach of the long arm of modern technology. He is a fitting symbol of culture and tradition having changed little through centuries of time.

It is difficult for outsiders to comprehend the closeness with which the pastoral peoples live with their domestic animals and the understanding and rapport they have with them. I have spent much time sitting quietly near a flock of goats or sheep listening to the shepherd directing their ways with a rich repertoire of clucks, hisses, trills and whistles. It is a communication refined by the

experience of centuries to which the animals respond with astonishing understanding.

A practical knowledge of botany was a prerequisite to survival for the pastoral peoples of the past, and it remains the same today for some. Nomadic Bedouin ladies are constantly searching the waysides, sorting and cutting, plucking up herbs of many kinds in due season and for specific purposes. I cannot help believing it would be a boon to each Middle Eastern university if such a lady were on their science staff, and how much America has lost because some Indian mothers were not reserved to serve in university botany departments.

But perhaps such a knowledge as these ladies possess cannot really be well learned unless the student lives close to the earth himself; unless he

147

The cedars have stood strong and changeless through history and today are lonely survivors of antiquity

Beyond a small grove of trees, clusters of purple lupine dapple an eastern mountain flank, an example of the profusion of springtime wildflowers fostered by three months of heavy winter rainfall.

feels and sees the subtle changes of the seasons; unless he sweats with the summer sun, wrinkles with the wind, and chills with the rainy season; and unless his very life depends upon the knowledge.

Connecting links

In an elevated setting, just beneath the crest of Lebanon's highest mountains, stands what is perhaps the most famous grove of trees in the world—the cedars of Lebanon. Because cedar wood resists weather well, has a pleasant aroma and because it became a symbol of power and longevity in the ancient world, King Solomon built his great temple in Jerusalem using these trees. But some specimens have stood strong and changeless through centuries of tumultuous history, and they stand today as peaceful patriarchs and lonely survivors of antiquity. If they had ears they would have heard both the rumble of war chariots and the screaming of modern jet fighter planes.

To receive the blessings of the cedars one must go up a narrow winding road beyond the market places, the noise, the smoke and the strife. The reward is worth the effort.

Above: *Chameleons and other lizards are plentiful.* Below: *Lebanon's blessings are symbolized by its fabled cedars. Ancient sentinels of the mountains, the cedars survive as testaments to the longevity and prosperity of this land.*

Foliose lichen is often found growing on the bark of a tree.

The Small World of LICHENS

By C. Boyd Pfeiffer
Photography by the Author

While lichens are known to many people who frequent the outdoors, most think of these plants only as the small, dull splotches seen on the exposed rocks of hillsides and cliffs. Dull they are for eyes five or six feet away, but they become miniature cascades of color when

en fruits of a dark crustose lichen often
ow on exposed rocks. From a distance this
hen looks black, and only with care can
ese red fruiting bodies be seen.

The goblet lichen, **Cladonia pyxidata,** is obviously named for its shape.

closely observed with the naked eye or with a magnifier. And the flattened splotches seen on bare rocks represent only a few of the estimated 15,000 species of lichens known to man.

Lichens are interesting members of the plant world in that each lichen is not one species of plant, but rather the combination of two plants —an alga and a fungus. To fully understand a lichen, we have to better understand the two plants involved. The fungus is the larger and more prominent of the two. All fungi depend upon the products of other plants for food and

LICHENS

nourishment. They completely lack chlorophyll and cannot manufacture their own food. Thus, all fungi live either as saprophytes, getting their nourishment from dead plants and animals, or as parasites, invading live plants and animals.

The fungus of a lichen gains carbohydrate nourishment from the alga and, in this sense, is parasitic, for it could not live without these products of the alga. However, the alga also benefits. The alga lives in layers a little below the surface of the lichen and is protected by it. Most algae live in water in ponds or streams. They cannot survive out of the water or stand the rigors of drying out. The alga in the lichen is no different but is protected from drying out and the hot rays of the sun by the protective shield of the outer surface of the fungus. The fungus, not requiring much water, supplies the alga with water and dissolved minerals in the water.

In structure lichens vary a great deal. In any lichen, of course, what one sees is a unified plant rather than the biological division of fungus and alga. There are several different types, depending upon their growing method. Those that the hiker scuffs with his feet on dry rocks are crustose or crusty varieties. These are flat and shapeless and may be colored gray, green, brown or black. Foliose lichens are those that are flat but leaflike, with free borders. More popularly they are called papery or leaflike lichens. Among the most beautiful are those with upright stems or stalks. Technically referred to as fruticose, they are also called stalked or shrubby lichens.

While the random-growing plant with its simple structure does not lend itself to any anatomical classification of parts, some general terms are used when discussing lichens. Usually the body of the plant itself is referred to as the thallus, except the fruiting portions that contain the spores. The outer skin is called the cortex, or outer rind. In some of the crustose lichens this is further subdivided into an upper rind and a lower rind, the latter having "holdfasts," or rhizoids, as extensions to hold the plants securely to a rock base.

Lichens do not have true roots and thus do not take in water with root hairs as some plants, but rather absorb it like a sponge. Also, they do not have stems, leaves, flowers or parts as other plants do, but the stalked lichens have

Reindeer moss, **Cladonia rangiferina,** grows on thin soil with other plants.

an upright stem called a podetium in the Cladonia species and a stipe in other species. It is at the apex of this stem that the fruiting bodies with their spores are found. The fruiting bodies are of two types: open fruit, called an apothecium; or closed fruit, called perithecium. The open-fruit type is shaped like a miniature cup with the spore layer completely exposed, while the closed-fruit type is like a round, closed sphere with a small pore through which the spores escape.

In **Cladonia cristatella**, the British soldier's crest or red-crest lichen, the fruiting bodies may be clearly seen. These may be red, maroon, black or even white.

The spores are contained in a small sack, usually eight to a sack. Furthermore, the spores of each individual species of lichen may vary a great deal in size, shape and structure and even the number of primary cells that make up the spore. Strangely enough, while a great deal of energy of the lichen goes into the production

of these fruiting bodies and spores, reproduction from spores is one of the least effective methods for the maintenance of the species. Although it is a common and effective means of reproduction in fungi such as the mushrooms, plant rusts, cup fungi, yeasts and others, it does not work well with lichens, because a lichen must have algal cells with it to gain nourishment.

Other forms of vegetative reproduction are far more common in lichens. Some lichens produce soredia, small dustlike particles which cover the surface of the lichen after being pushed up from the deeper cells of the plant. These contain small filamentous strands of the fungal portion of the lichen surrounding a few algal cells. The soredia are gradually knocked off the plant, carried by the wind or by animals to other areas, where they begin production of new lichens. Similar to this is the spreading of lichens by the breaking up of the plant into smaller pieces containing both alga and fungus. The hiker who scrapes his feet across a granite boulder may well be breaking off parts of lichen and indirectly contributing to the spreading and welfare of that particular species.

Lichens benefit both man and animals. Caribou and reindeer have fed for ages on the lichen of the frozen north, *Cladonia rangiferina*. Commonly called reindeer moss, *Cladonia rangiferina* is not a moss at all, but a spongy, moss-like, silver-gray lichen with brown fruiting bodies. Rock tripes, a form of foliose lichen, are eaten in Japan.

The yarn of genuine Harris Tweeds is still colored with dyes made by lichens leached in human urine. Litmus paper, known to every high school chemistry student as a test paper for acid and alkaline substances, is made from a lichen species. Lichens have also gone into tanning agents and have been used in medicinal products in the past.

Where are lichens found? Everywhere. They live on rocks, poor soil, tree bark, dead wood and sometimes even on other lichens. They frequent out-of-the-way places, trails, wilderness areas and high cliffs. About the only place they are not found is in cities or in air-polluted areas. For the hiker, the nature lover, the naturalist, the frequenter of out-of-the-way places, a close look at lichens provides a glimpse of a small world of beauty and a closer understanding of a basic form of life.

The Scotch bonnet feeds mainly on sea urchins; the banded tulip feeds on clams and bubble shells.

Gifts from the Sea

The sand bars, mud flats and inlets of Cape Romano offer over 350 kinds of shells to collectors

By Emma Mae Chew
Photography by Neal Leeman

Porpoises leap on all sides as we skim across the smooth waters of Gullivan Bay. Cape Romano, the northernmost outpost of the legendary Ten Thousand Islands on Florida's southwest coast, is visible on the horizon.

We watch eagerly for the first glimpse of the Gulf. It may be in a gentle mood, or tossing its treasures upon the shore with a mighty surge. This bit of land edged with fine white sand draws us like a magnet.

Shells are piled in profusion along the shore. Dainty rose petals, yellow cockles, elegant lucinas, large heart cockles, ponderous arks and turkey wings are picked up with the hinges intact. We reach for a speckled Chinese alphabet or lettered olive before it rolls back

into the water as the wave recedes. Along the tide line golden yellow buttercup halves are filled with sea water.

Hundreds of iridescent pen shells have been tossed high onto the beach. Lace and apple murex are welcome finds. Many halves of jingle, or baby-footprint, shells are shifted by the waves, their silvery colors of orange, gold and black glistening in the sunlight. They make a pleasant jingling sound when several are bounced together.

Dainty coquinas live in the sand at tide line. They burrow into the sand as the wave recedes faster than we can dig them up. Their pastel colors with radiating and plaid designs resemble tiny butterflies.

Pectens flit through the tide pools and shallows near shore, snapping their two valves together and ejecting a stream of water that propels them forward sometimes a yard or more. This creature has as many as 120 eyes that rim the edge of the double-fringed mantle and sparkle like diamonds when the mantle waves in the water.

A rare find along the shore is the aristocratic junonia, its spindle shape marked with brown and orange spots on creamy white. It lives in deep water and is sometimes found after a storm has stirred up the ocean depths.

At low tide we search the sand bars, mud flats and exposed inlets for specimens, and we find a banded tulip feeding on a bubble shell. A powerful horse conch has attacked a clam, and a king's crown feasts on a murex.

Large clams betray their hiding places under the sand by shooting a stream of water into the air. The young shells have streaks resembling lightning zigzagging over the tan

Tracks are left by the lettered olives when they push through the sand feeding on smaller mollusks.

color. Their egg cases are long, spiraling strings of flat parchmentlike capsules.

The moon snail makes a strange egg case called a sand collar. The snail pushes a sheet of mucus out from under its foot and molds the collar on the surface of its round shell.

We dig in the mud flats for sunray shells whose lines radiate from the hinge to the valve edge like the rays of the setting sun. The polished tan or brown shells grow to an oblong length of five or six inches.

In the peat beds and inlets we look for signs of the lovely, fragile angel wings, but these beautiful creatures stay hidden from view. They are able to burrow deeply into the mud and then reach the sea water with a long siphon. When we find these siphons, we quickly dig for the treasure beneath. In peat beds along the shoreline we uncover hundreds of dainty white false angel wings from one-quarter inch to two inches in length.

On the sand bars ribbon-like tracks lead us to uncovering a sand dollar as thin as a wafer. The highly polished lettered olives push their way up through the sand and make tracks as they glide along. On the rise of the tide, surf clams and sunrays pop up through the sand.

Hundreds of gulls, pelicans and sandpipers are feeding the sand bar, and, as we draw near, they soar into the air and circle around to make a landing on another exposed area. The tiny sandpipers seem to have only one leg as they hop along. Then their toothpick legs move so rapidly that they become a blur before the take-off. The cormorants come in for a fast landing. Using their feet against the water as a brake, they slide along with their heads back and bills pointed upward.

The inlet at Morgan Pass is a favorite camping place. We try not to disturb the pink roseate spoonbills feeding on the mud flats. Along the shore we are still tempted to bend over, for scattered here and there are boat shells, kitten paws, bubbles, paper figs, sea urchins, nutmegs, and scotch bonnets. But hunger and weariness are upon us, so we build a campfire and relax around its cherry glow. As the potatoes roast, we look over our treasures and agree with Robert Louis Stevenson who said, "It is perhaps a more fortunate destiny to have a taste for collecting shells than to be born a millionaire."

About this time of the evening in June and July the large loggerhead turtles emerge from

The Cabrit's murex is characterized by attractive spines and frills.

the Gulf waters and lumber over the sand to make their nests and bury their eggs. They dig a hole two or three feet deep and deposit from a hundred to one hundred and sixty eggs, cover them over with sand and return to the sea. Their flippers make deep tracks in the sand to and from the nest, the tracks remaining until washed away by waves or rain.

As the evening shadows deepen, we view the brilliant lights appearing as jewels flung high in the sky. Under this canopy of splendor, we close our eyes. The call of chuck-will's-widow and the rhythm of the waves lull us to sleep as a soft gentle breeze brushes our faces.

Before leaving we must visit "our island," a small sandbar within sight of the southern most tip of Cape Romano that has been growing and nurturing life for several years — different kinds of life with each change of tide and shift of the trade winds that sweep over it. We have found refuge in its horseshoe curve when fleeing from an unexpected storm.

The graceful least terns hover over the island filling the air with their calls. Their nests are nothing more than a curved spot in the sand hollowed out by the mother tern's breast. The spot chosen so closely resembles the grey and white speckled eggs that we almost step on the eggs and newly hatched young before we see them. Suddenly a great white heron settles on the highest ridge of broken shells and seems to rest and meditate.

The gentle porpoises escort us on our return trip through Gullivan Bay. In the top of a mangrove tree an osprey is setting on its nest of sticks. A magnificent frigate bird glides into a white cloud high above us, and a bald eagle floats down to light in the tallest Australian pine.

At the boat landing we tell an old-timer that we have collected over eighty species of shells in two days.

"You have a long way to go. Over 350 different kinds of shells have been found here," is his reply.

With our gifts from the sea and the cry of the gulls and least terns ringing in our ears, we turn homeward. The same problems are waiting, but we have found new strength to cope with them.

Sozon's cone is one of the uncommon species found in tropical waters of the Americas.

nature's erupting statues

by Leonard E. Foote / Photography by the Author

If man finds life in space, it may be in a mushroom spore. For mushroom spores are orbiting travelers, rising on thermals to the jet streams of the upper atmosphere, to fall, germinate and send up dainty parasols from the arctics to the tropics. Some of the most delightful displays of these erupting statues may be observed in the southern mountains, U.S.A.

Many of the 1,000 kinds of southern mountain mushrooms occur throughout the world, and Swedish handbooks are almost as useful to identify mushrooms at Asheville or Seattle as they are at Stockholm. One may purchase the imported chanterelle—a gourmet's delight—in a downtown delicatessen, or gather this native, bright orange mushroom by the bushel after a southern Appalachian summer rain. Yet, often these plants of high color and varied form are unnoticed by campers, bird students, amateur photographers and other woods walkers. They don't know what they are missing.

Mushrooms were savory delicacies to the Roman Caesars. Nero and Claudius possessed slaves solely to search out delicate mushrooms for Roman feasts, or lethal specimens for quiet elimination of aspiring enemies. Although the Roman consuls thought mushrooms originated from the "ferment of the earth," they admired their graceful form as well as their culinary properties.

In damp laurel slicks along Appalachian streams, where rainfall annually exceeds 50 to 85 inches, colorful toadstools (a name used interchangeably with mushrooms, but sometimes referring to the poisonous or non-edible varieties) may erupt every month of the year. During July,

Dry Marasmius   Chlorine Amanita

the vivid red-capped russulas—the mushroom said to have poisoned Czar Alexis—will be found pushing through the verdant mosses lining the forest floor. With the russulas will be the vermillion chanterelle, the dry marasmius or the brown-spored, web-bearing cortinarius.

Approximately 35 species of the collybia, a small coin mushroom, are found in the Appalachians, growing on the roots of pine and oak trees. At night one may see the oak-leaved forest floor lighted from the flourescent glow of the jack-o-lantern mushrooms.

In dryer situations, summer rains bring on a flowering of mushrooms. On oak- and pine-covered hillsides, after a summer soaking, the leaf litter will explode with latex-bearing lactariuses, which exude fluid when broken.

Among them will be statuesque amanitas, some poisonous, some edible, but all showy. In similar forests near Rome, it was the delicious *Amanita caesaria* the emperors' slaves sought. Modern mushroom pickers know it as Caesar's mushroom. This fragile yellow-to-red-capped parasol quickly completes its progenesis: if it springs from the leaf litter at sunrise to shed its spores, it begins decaying by the next sunset.

Often growing with the Caesar's is the destroying angel, a chiseling in alabaster so toxic that eating a half-inch cube will cause delirium, severe illness and often death. In France, where a national mushroom show is held annually, poisoning from the albuminous phallin of the European version of this death cup is such a common toxication that the Pasteur Institute developed an anti-phallin serum. French law requires that the serum be stocked by physicians in all sections of the country.

Aztec Indians in Mexico used a sacred mushroom as a narcotic in religious ceremonies; and certain native tribes in Siberia concoct an intoxicating liquor from the fly amanita, a red-capped and textured—and dangerous—beauty one may encounter in the southern United States.

The bolete mushroom, whose spores are produced in pores rather than gills, is common throughout America, as is the lepiota which is a golf course and lawn mushroom. The lepiota is

Chanterelle

Edible

Caesar's
Mushroom

Fly
Amanita

Poisonous

Destroying
Angel

nature's erupting statues

almost always found on new lawns where the soil is rich.

The amanitopsis, a summer mushroom, often appears a year or two after a forest has been logged.

The edible morel, which grows mostly in spring and summer, is highly prized by gourmets. It thrives on the north slopes of hardwood forests, and other wooded areas.

Mushrooms also abound in pastures and fields or may spring up overnight on a meticulously manicured lawn. Few city parks or recreation areas are without mushrooms during the year, and even Central Park in New York City has a varied mushroom flora.

Mushrooms are grandiose fungi, grossly unlike the humble rusts and molds which are their close kin. The fruiting body often seems to pop up almost overnight—observe the familiar fairy rings—but the mushroom may have been growing for weeks. With the first warm days of spring, mushroom spores swell and push out threadlike strands through the leaf litter and soil. This web of silken filaments solicits organic matter and moisture finally to coalesce and suddenly bring forth the complex mushroom inflorescence. Most fungi are saprophytes—plants feeding on organic matter—and possess no chlorophyll, as do algae and the green higher plants, to synthesize foods from carbon, air and water.

To complete the life cycle, spores are formed on club-shaped basidia: in gilled mushrooms, myriads of minute basidia line the gill walls, looking like stacks of baseball bats. Each basidium shoots off four spores with sufficient velocity to escape between the gill filaments and be borne away by gentle air currents.

A spore print from a mushroom cap left on a sheet of paper in a draft-free area for ten hours or more will mirror the gill pattern and disclose the color of the spore mass, an important characteristic in identification. To perpetuate its kind, a medium-sized field mushroom ejects billions of spores during its few hours to days of maturity.

Many animals beside man relish the taste of a mushroom. Spotted skunks, moles, shrews, squirrels, grouse, turtles and even armadillos eat mushrooms. The deer of the Ocala National Forest in Florida are the mushroom gourmets of the animal world. Parasoled fungi growing among the pines in the hammocks and flats furnish a major portion of the deer's diet in this national forest.

Mushrooms are artistic subjects for amateur lensmen armed with high-speed color films and the inexpensive closeup devices now available for most cameras. Quality portraits of honey-colored parasols growing in deep woods can be made with the help of small foil-covered cardboards, much in the same manner a portrait photographer highlights chestnut tresses of the local beauty queen.

But to those amateur naturalists who would emulate the Roman Caesars by testing a Caesar's amanita on a sirloin, all mushroom experts give standard warning: eat only mushrooms you can identify positively as edible, else you may hear in your delirium the siren song of the marble-white destroying angel.

Collybia

Bolete

Lepiota